Virgil, Alfred John Church, Bartolomeo Pinelli

Stories from Virgil

Virgil, Alfred John Church, Bartolomeo Pinelli

Stories from Virgil

ISBN/EAN: 9783337006129

Printed in Europe, USA, Canada, Australia, Japan

Cover: Foto ©Thomas Meinert / pixelio.de

More available books at **www.hansebooks.com**

THE FLIGHT FROM TROY.

STORIES FROM VIRGIL

BY THE

REV. ALFRED J. CHURCH, M.A.

Head Master of King Edward's School, Retford;

AUTHOR OF "STORIES FROM HOMER."

WITH TWENTY-FOUR ILLUSTRATIONS

FROM PINELLI'S DESIGNS

NEW YORK:

SCRIBNER AND WELFORD.

1879.

CONTENTS.

I *

LIST OF ILLUSTRATIONS.

TO THE HONOURED MEMORY

OF

JOHN CONINGTON

THIS BOOK IS DEDICATED.

PREFACE.

THE favour with which the public received "Stories from Homer" has encouraged me to deal in the same way with the Æneid. I have found it a difficult task, and I must ask the indulgence of my readers, who will certainly miss, not only the freshness and simplicity of the great Greek epic, but those chief characteristics of Virgil, his supreme mastery of expression and the splendour of his style. I beg them to remember that I do not attempt to translate my original, that while I add nothing (except, in a very few instances, an explanatory phrase), I am constrained to leave out much ; and that what I leave out, or, at the most, very inadequately render, will often be found to be that which they have been accustomed most to admire in the poet,—his brilliant rhetoric, his philosophy, his imagination, and his pathos. My chief aim has been to represent to English readers the narrative, the interest of which is, perhaps, scarcely appreciated.

The illustrations (with the exception of the second, which is taken from a photograph of the antique) have been adapted from a series of designs, published early in this century, by Pinelli, a Roman artist (1781–1835), who acquired a considerable reputation among his countrymen, especially for the power of representing energetic action. I may be allowed to express my great obligations to the pains and skill (to which indeed this volume is otherwise much indebted) which have been used in making these designs available for the present purpose.

RETFORD,
September 25, 1878.

STORIES FROM VIRGIL.

CHAPTER I.

THE HORSE OF WOOD.

FOR ten years King Agamemnon and the men
of Greece laid siege to Troy. But though sentence had gone forth against the city, yet the
day of its fall tarried, because certain of the gods
loved it well and defended it, as Apollo, and
Mars, the God of war, and Father Jupiter himself. Wherefore Minerva put it into the heart
of Epeius, Lord of the Isles, that he should make
a cunning device wherewith to take the city.
Now the device was this: he made a great
Horse of wood, feigning it to be a peace offering
to Minerva, that the Greeks might have a safe
return to their homes. In the belly of this
there hid themselves certain of the bravest of
the chiefs, as Menelaüs, and Ulysses, and Thoas

2

the Ætolian, and Machaon, the great physician, and Pyrrhus son of Achilles (but Achilles himself was dead, slain by Paris, Apollo helping, even as he was about to take the city), and others also, and with them Epeius himself. But the rest of the people made as if they had departed to their homes ; only they went not further than Tenedos, which was an island near to the coast.

Great joy was there in Troy when it was noised abroad that the men of Greece had departed. The gates were opened, and the people went forth to see the plain and the camp. And one said to another, as they went, "Here they set the battle in array, and there were the tents of the fierçe Achilles, and there lay the ships." And some stood and marvelled at the great peace-offering to Minerva, even the Horse of wood. And Thymœtes, who was one of the elders of the city, was the first who advised that it should be brought within the walls and set in the citadel. But whether he gave this counsel out of a false heart, or because the Gods would have it so, no man knows. And Capys, and others with him, said that it should be drowned in water, or burned with fire, or that men should pierce it and see whether there were aught within. And the people were divided, some crying one thing and some another. Then came forward the priest Laocoön, and a great company with him, crying, "What madness is this? Think ye that the men of Greece are indeed departed, or that there is any profit in their gifts? Surely, there are armed men in this mighty Horse; or haply they have made it that they may look down upon our walls. Touch it not, for as for these men of Greece, I fear them, even though they bring gifts in their hands."

And as he spake he cast his great spear at the Horse, so that it sounded again. But the Gods would not that Troy should be saved.

Meanwhile there came certain shepherds, dragging with them one whose hands were bound behind his back. He had come forth to them, they said, of his own accord, when they were in the field. And first the young men gathered about him mocking him, but when he cried aloud, "What place is left for me, for the Greeks suffer me not to live, and the men of Troy cry for vengeance upon me?" they rather pitied him, and bade him speak, and say whence he came and what he had to tell.

Then the man spake, turning to King Priam : " I will speak the truth, whatever befall me. My name is Sinon, and I deny not that I am a Greek. Haply thou hast heard the name of Palamedes, whom the Greeks slew, but now, being dead, lament; and the cause was that, because he counselled peace, men falsely accused him of treason. Now, of this Palamedes I was a poor kinsman, and followed him to Troy. And when he was dead, through the false witness of Ulysses, I lived in great grief and trouble, nor could I hold my peace, but sware that if ever I came back to Argos I would avenge me of him that had done this deed. Then did Ulysses seek occasion against me, whispering evil things, nor rested till at the last, Calchas the soothsayer helping him—but what profit it that I should tell these things ? For doubtless ye hold one Greek to be even as another. Wherefore slay me, and doubtless ye will do a pleasure to Ulysses and the sons of Atreus."

Then they bade him tell on, and he said,—

" Often would the Greeks have fled to their

homes, being weary of the war, but still the stormy sea hindered them. And when this Horse that ye see had been built, most of all did the dreadful thunder roll from the one end of the heaven to the other. Then the Greeks sent one who should inquire of Apollo; and Apollo answered them thus: 'Men of Greece, even as ye appeased the winds with blood when ye came to Troy, so must ye appease them with blood now that ye would go from thence.' Then did men tremble to think on whom the doom should fall, and Ulysses, with much clamour, drew forth Calchas the soothsayer into the midst, and bade him say who it was that the Gods would have as a sacrifice. Then did many forebode evil for me. Ten days did the soothsayer keep silence, saying that he would not give any one to death. But then, for in truth the two had planned the matter beforehand, he spake, appointing me to die. And to this thing they all agreed, each being glad to turn to another that which he feared for himself. But when the day was come, and all things were ready, the salted meal for the sacrifice and the garlands, lo! I burst my

bonds and fled, and hid myself in the sedges of
a pool, waiting till they should have set sail, if
haply that might be.   But never shall I see
country, or father, or children again.   For
doubtless on these will they take vengeance
for my flight.   Only do thou, O king, have pity
on me, who have suffered many things, and yet
have harmed no man."

And King Priam had pity on him, and bade
them loose his bonds, saying, "Whoever thou
art, forget now thy country.   Henceforth thou
art one of us.   But tell me true : why made
they this huge Horse ?   Who contrived it ?
What seek they by it ? to please the Gods or
to further their siege ?"

Then said Sinon, and as he spake he
stretched his hands to the sky, "I call you to
witness, ye everlasting fires of heaven, that
with good right I now break my oath of fealty
and reveal the secrets of my countrymen.
Listen then, O king.   All our hope has ever
been in the help of Minerva.   But, from the
day when Diomed and Ulysses dared, having
bloody hands, to snatch her image from her
holy place in Troy, her face was turned from

us. Well do I remember how the eyes of the
image, well-nigh before they had set it in the
camp, blazed with wrath, and how the salt
sweat stood upon its limbs, aye, and how it thrice
leapt from the ground, shaking shield and spear.
Then Calchas told us that we must cross the
seas again, and seek at home fresh omens
for our war. And this, indeed, they are doing
even now, and will return anon. Also the
soothsayer said, ' Meanwhile ye must make
the likeness of a Horse, to be a peace-offering to
Minerva. And take heed that ye make it huge
of bulk, so that the men of Troy may not receive it into their gates, nor bring it within
their walls, and get safety for themselves
thereby. For if,' he said, ' the men of Troy
harm this image at all, they shall surely perish ;
but if they bring it into their city, then shall
Asia lay siege hereafter to the city of Pelops,
and our children shall suffer the doom which
we would fain have brought on Troy.' "

These words wrought much on the men of
Troy, and as they pondered on them, lo! the
Gods sent another marvel to deceive them.
For while Laocoön, the priest of Neptune, was

slaying a bull at the altar of his god, there came two serpents across the sea from Tenedos, whose heads and necks, whereon were thick manes of hair, were high above the waves, and many scaly coils trailed behind in the waters. And when they reached the land they still sped forward. Their eyes were red as blood and blazed with fire, and their forked tongues hissed loud for rage. Then all the men of Troy grew pale with fear and fled away, but these turned not aside this way or that, seeking Laocoön where he stood. And first they wrapped themselves about his little sons, one serpent about each, and began to devour them. And when the father would have given help to his children, having a sword in his hand, they seized upon himself, and bound him fast with their folds. Twice they compassed about his body, and twice his neck, lifting their heads far above him. And all the while he strove to tear them away with his hands, his priest's garlands dripping with blood. Nor did he cease to cry horribly aloud, even as a bull bellows when after an ill stroke of the axe it flees from the altar. But when their work was done, the two glided

LAOCOON.

to the citadel of Minerva, and hid themselves
beneath the feet and the shield of the goddess.
And men said one to another, "Lo! the priest
Laocoön has been judged according to his
deeds; for he cast his spear against this holy
thing, and now the Gods have slain him." Then
all cried out together that the Horse of wood
must be drawn to the citadel. Whereupon they
opened the Scæan Gate, and pulled down the
wall that was thereby, and put rollers under the
feet of the Horse, and joined ropes thereto. So,
in much joy, they drew it into the city, youths
and maidens singing about it the while, and
laying their hands to the ropes with great glad-
ness. And yet there wanted not signs and
tokens of evil to come. Four times it halted
on the threshold of the gate, and men might
have heard a clashing of arms within. Cassandra also opened her mouth, prophesying
evil: but no man heeded her, for that was ever
the doom upon her, not to be believed speaking
truth. So the men of Troy drew the Horse
into the city. And that night they kept a feast
to all the Gods with great joy, not knowing that
the last day of the great city had come.

CHAPTER II.

BUT when night was now fully come, and the men of Troy lay asleep, lo! from the ship of King Agamemnon there rose up a flame for a signal to the Greeks; and these straightway manned their ships, and made across the sea from Tenedos, there being a great calm, and the moon also giving them light. Sinon likewise opened a secret door that was in the great Horse, and the chiefs issued forth therefrom, and opened the gates of the city, slaying those that kept watch.

Meanwhile there came a vision to Æneas, who now, Hector being dead, was the chief hope and stay of the men of Troy. It was Hector's self that he seemed to see, but not such as he had seen him coming back rejoicing with the arms of Achilles, or setting fire to the ships, but even as he lay after that Achilles dragged him at his chariot wheels, covered with dust and blood, his feet swollen and pierced through with thongs. To him said Æneas, not knowing what he said, "Why hast thou tarried so long ? Much have we suffered waiting for thee ! And what grief hath marked thy face ? and whence these wounds ? "

But to this the spirit answered nothing, but said, groaning the while, "Fly, son of Venus, fly, and save thee from these flames. The enemy is in the walls, and Troy hath utterly perished. If any hand could have saved our city, this hand had done so. Thou art now the hope of Troy. Take then her Gods, and flee with them for company, seeking the city that thou shalt one day build across the sea."

And now the alarm of battle came nearer and nearer, and Æneas, waking from sleep, climbed upon the roof, and looked on the city. As a shepherd stands, and sees a fierce flame sweeping before the south wind over the corn-fields or a flood rushing down from the mountains, so he stood. And as he looked, the great palace of Deïphobus sank down in the fire, and the house of Ucalegon, that was hard by, blazed forth, till the sea by Sigeüm shone with the light. Then, scarce knowing what he sought, he girded on his armour, thinking, perchance, that he might yet win some place of vantage, or, at the least, might avenge himself on the enemy, or find honour in his death. But as he passed from out of his house there met him Panthus, the priest of Apollo that was on the citadel, who cried to him, "O Æneas, the glory is departed from Troy, and the Greeks have the mastery in the city; for armed men are coming forth from the great Horse of wood, and thousands also swarm in at the gates, which Sinon hath treacherously opened." And as he spake others came up under the light of the moon, as Hypanis, and Dymas, and young Corœbus, who had but newly come to Troy, seeking Cassandra to be his wife. To whom Æneas spake: "If ye are minded, my brethren, to follow me to the death, come on. For how things fare this night ye see. The Gods who were the stay of this city have departed from it; nor is aught remaining to which we may bring succour. Yet can we die as brave men in battle. And haply he that counts his life to be lost may yet save it." Then, even as ravening wolves hasten through the mist seeking for prey, so they went through the city, doing dreadful deeds. And for a while the men of Greece fled before them.

First of all there met them Androgeos with a great company following him, who, thinking them to be friends, said, " Haste, comrades, why are ye so late ? We are spoiling this city of Troy, and ye are but newly come from the ships." But forthwith, for they answered him not as he had looked for, he knew that he had fallen among enemies. Then even as one who treads upon a snake unawares among thorns, and flies from it when it rises angrily against him with swelling neck, so Androgeos would have fled. But the men of Troy rushed on, and, seeing that they knew all the place, and that great fear was upon the Greeks, slew many men. Then said Corœbus, "We have good luck in this matter, my friends. Come now, let us change our shields, and put upon us the armour of these Greeks. For whether we deal with our enemy by craft or by force, who will ask ?" Then he took to himself the helmet and shield of Androgeos, and also girded his sword

upon him.   In like manner did the others, and
thus going disguised among the Greeks slew
many, so that some again fled to the ships and
some were fain to climb into the Horse of wood.
But lo! men came dragging by the hair from
the temple of Minerva the virgin Cassandra,
whom when Corœbus beheld, and how she
lifted up her eyes to heaven (but as for her
hands, they were bound with iron), he endured
not the sight, but threw himself upon those that
dragged her, the others following him.   Then
did a grievous mischance befall them, for the
men of Troy that stood upon the roof of the
temple cast spears against them, judging them
to be enemies.   The Greeks also, being wroth
that the virgin should be taken from them,
fought the more fiercely, and many who had
before been put to flight in the city came
against them, and prevailed, being indeed many
against few.   Then first of all fell Corœbus, being
slain by Peneleus the Bœotian, and Rhipeus
also, the most righteous of all the sons of Troy.
But the Gods dealt not with him after his
righteousness.   Hypanis also was slain and
Dymas, and Panthus escaped not for all that

more than other men he feared the Gods and
was also the priest of Apollo.

Then was Æneas severed from the rest,
having with him two only, Iphitus and Pelias,
Iphitus being an old man and Pelias sorely
wounded by Ulysses. And these, hearing a
great shouting, hastened to the palace of King
Priam, where the battle was fiercer than in any
place beside. For some of the Greeks were
seeking to climb the walls, laying ladders thereto, whereon they stood, holding forth their
shields with their left hands, and with their right
grasping the roofs. And the men of Troy, on
the other hand, being in the last extremity, tore
down the battlements and the gilded beams
wherewith the men of old had adorned the
palace. Then Æneas, knowing of a secret door
whereby the unhappy Andromaché in past days
had been wont to enter, bringing her son
Astyanax to his grandfather, climbed on to the
roof, and joined himself to those that fought therefrom. Now upon this roof there was a tower,
whence all Troy could be seen, and the camp
of the Greeks and the ships. This the men of
Troy loosened from its foundations with bars

of iron, and thrust it over, so that it fell upon
the enemy, slaying many of them. But not the
less did others press forward, casting the while
stones and javelins and all that came to their
hands.

Meanwhile others sought to break down the
gates of the palace, Pyrrhus, son of Achilles,
being foremost among them, clad in shining
armour of bronze. Like to a serpent was he,
which sleeps indeed during the winter, but in
the spring comes forth into the light, full fed
on evil herbs, and, having cast his skin and
renewed his youth, lifts his head into the light
of the sun and hisses with forked tongue. And
with Pyrrhus were tall Periphas, and Autome-
don, who had been armour-bearer to his father
Achilles, and following them the youth of Scyros,
which was the kingdom of his grandfather
Lycomedes. With a great battle-axe he hewed
through the doors, breaking down also the door-
posts, though they were plated with bronze,
making, as it were, a great window, through
which a man might see the palace within, the
hall of King Priam, and of the kings who had
reigned aforetime in Troy. But when they that

were within perceived it, there arose a great cry
of women wailing aloud and clinging to the
doors and kissing them. But ever Pyrrhus
pressed on, fierce and strong as ever was his
father Achilles, nor could aught stand against
him, either the doors or they that guarded them.
Then, as a river bursts its banks and overflows
the plain, so did the sons of Greece rush into
the palace.

But old Priam, when he saw the enemy in his
hall, girded on him his armour, which now by
reason of old age he had long laid aside, and
took a spear in his hand, and would have gone
against the adversary, only Queen Hecuba
called to him from where she sat. For she and
her daughters had fled to the great altar of the
household Gods, and sat crowded about it like
unto doves that are driven by a storm. Now
the altar stood in an open court that was in the
midst of the palace, with a great bay-tree above
it. So when she saw Priam, how he had girded
himself with armour as a youth, she cried to
him and said, " What hath bewitched thee, that
thou girdest thyself with armour ? It is not the
sword that shall help us this day ; no, not though

3

my own Hector were here, but rather the Gods
and their altars.   Come hither to us, for here
thou wilt be safe, or at the least wilt die with
us."

So she made the old man sit down in the
midst.   But lo! there came flying through the
palace, Polites, his son, wounded to death by the
spear of Pyrrhus, and Pyrrhus close behind him.
And he, even as he came into the sight of his
father and his mother, fell dead upon the ground.
But when King Priam saw it he contained not
himself, but cried aloud, "Now may the gods, if
there be any justice in heaven, recompense thee
for this wickedness, seeing that thou hast not
spared to slay the son before his father's eyes.
Great Achilles, whom thou falsely callest thy sire,
did not thus to Priam, though he was an enemy,
but reverenced right and truth, and gave the
body of Hector for burial, and sent me back to
my city."

And as he spake the old man cast a spear,
but aimless and without force, and that pierced
not even the boss of the shield.   Then said the
son of Achilles, " Go thou and tell my father of
his unworthy son and all these evil deeds.   And

that thou mayest tell him, die!" And as he spake he caught in his left hand the old man's white hair, and dragged him, slipping the while in the blood of his own son, to the altar, and then, lifting his sword high for a blow, drave it to the hilt in the old man's side. So King Priam, who had ruled mightily over many peoples and countries in the land of Asia, was slain that night, having first seen Troy burning about him, and his citadel laid even with the ground. So was his carcass cast out upon the earth, headless, and without a name.

CHAPTER III.

ALL these things, indeed, Æneas beheld, but could not bear help, being one against many. But when the deed was done, and the old man lay dead, he bethought him of his father Anchises, and his wife Creüsa, and of his little son Ascanius, and how he had left them without defence at home. But as he turned to seek them, the night being now, by reason of many fires, as clear as the day, he espied Helen sitting in the temple of Vesta, where she had sought sanctuary; for she feared the men of Troy, to whom she had brought ruin and destruction, and not less her own husband, whom she had deceived. Then was his wrath kindled, and he spake to himself, "Shall this evil woman return safe to Sparta? Shall she see again her home and her children, with Trojan women forsooth to be her handmaidens? Shall Troy be burnt and King

Priam be slain, and she take no harm? Not
so; for though there be no glory to be won from
such a deed, yet shall I satisfy myself, taking
vengeance upon her for my kinsmen and my
countrymen." But while he thought these
things in his heart, lo! there appeared unto
him Venus, his mother, made manifest as he
had never seen her before, as fair and as tall as
the dwellers in heaven behold her. Then
Venus spake thus, "What meaneth all this
rage, my son? Hast thou no care for me?
Hast thou forgotten thy father Anchises, and
thy wife, and thy little son? Of a surety the
fire and the sword had consumed them long
since but that I cared for them and saved them.
It is not Helen; no, nor Paris, that hath laid
low this great city of Troy, but the wrath of the
Gods. See now, for I will take away the mist
that covers thine eyes; see how Neptune with
his trident is overthrowing the walls and root-
ing up the city from its foundations; and how
Juno stands with spear and shield in the Scæan
Gate, and calls fresh hosts from the ships; and
how Pallas sits on the height with the storm-
cloud about her and her Gorgon shield; and

how Father Jupiter himself stirs up the enemy
against Troy.   Fly, therefore, my son.   I will
not leave thee till thou shalt reach thy father's
house."   And as she spake she vanished in the
darkness.

Then did Æneas see dreadful forms and
Gods who were the enemies of Troy, and before
his eyes the whole city seemed to sink down
into the fire.   Even as a mountain oak upon
the hills on which the woodmen ply their
axes bows its head while all its boughs shake
about it, till at last, as blow comes after blow,
with a mighty groan it falls crashing down
from the height, even so the city seemed to fall.
Then did Æneas pass on his way, the goddess
leading him, and the flames gave place to him,
and the javelins harmed him not.

But when he was come to his house he bethought him first of the old man his father; but
when he would have carried him to the hills,
Anchises would not, being loath to live in some
strange country when Troy had perished.
" Nay," said he, " fly ye who are strong and in
the flower of your days.   But as for me, if the
Gods had willed that I should live, they had saved

this dwelling for me. Enough is it, yea, and more than enough, that once I have seen this city taken, and lived. Bid me, then, farewell as though I were dead. Death will I find for myself. And truly I have long lingered here a useless stock and hated of the Gods since Jupiter smote me with the blast of his thunder."

Nor could the old man be moved from his purpose, though his son and his son's wife, and even the child Ascanius, besought him with many tears that he should not make yet heavier the doom that was upon them. Then was Æneas minded to go back to the battle and die. For what hope was left? "Thoughtest thou, my father," he cried, "that I should flee and leave thee behind? What evil word is this that has fallen from thy lips? If the Gods will have it that nought of Troy should be left, and thou be minded that thou and thine should perish with the city, be it so. The way is easy; soon will Pyrrhus be here; Pyrrhus, red with Priam's blood; Pyrrhus, who slays the son before the face of the father, and the father at the altar. Was it for this, kind Mother Venus, that thou broughtest me safe through fire and sword, to

see the enemy in my home, and my father and
my wife and my son lying slaughtered together?
Comrades, give me my arms, and take me back
to the battle.   At the least I will die avenged."

But as he girded on his arms and would have
departed from the house, his wife Creüsa caught
his feet upon the threshold, staying him, and
held out the little Ascanius, saying, " If thou
goest to thy death, take wife and child with
thee; but if thou hopest aught from arms, guard
first the house where thou hast father and wife
and child."

And lo! as she spake there befell a mighty
marvel, for before the face of father and mother
there was seen to shine a light on the head of
the boy Ascanius, and to play upon his waving
hair and glitter on his temples. And when they
feared to see this thing, and would have stifled
the flame or quenched it with water, the old man
Anchises in great joy raised his eyes to heaven,
and cried aloud, "O Father Jupiter, if prayer
move thee at all, give thine aid and make this
omen sure." And even as he spake the thunder
rolled on his left hand, and a star shot through
the skies, leaving a long trail of light behind,

and passed over the house-tops till it was hidden in the woods of Ida. Then the old man lifted himself up and did obeisance to the star, and said, " I delay no more : whithersoever ye lead I will follow. Gods of my country, save my house and my grandson. This omen is of you. And now, my son, I refuse not to go."

Then said Æneas, and as he spake the fire came nearer, and the light was clearer to see, and the heat more fierce, " Climb, dear father, on my shoulders ; I will bear thee, nor grow weary with the weight. We will be saved or perish together. The little Ascanius shall go with me, and my wife follow behind, not over near. And ye, servants of my house, hearken to me ; ye mind how that to one who passes out of the city there is a tomb and a temple of Ceres in a lonely place, and an ancient cypress-tree hard by. There will we gather by divers ways. And do thou, my father, take the holy images in thy hands, for as for me, who have but newly come from battle, I may not touch them till I have washed me in the running stream."

And as he spake he put a cloak of lion's skin upon his shoulders, and the old man sat thereon.

Ascanius also laid hold of his hand, and Creüsa
followed behind. So he went in much dread and
trembling. For indeed before sword and spear of
the enemy he had not feared, but now he feared for
them that were with him. But when he was come
nigh unto the gates, and the journey was well-
nigh finished, there befell a grievous mischance,
for there was heard a sound as of many feet
through the darkness; and the old man cried to
him, " Fly, my son, fly; they are coming. I see
the flashing of shields and swords." But as
Æneas hasted to go, Creüsa his wife was severed
from him. But whether she wandered from the
way or sat down in weariness, no man may say.
Only he saw her no more, nor knew her to be
lost till, all his company being met at the temple
of Ceres, she only was found wanting. Very
grievous did the thing seem to him, nor did he
cease to cry out in his wrath against Gods and
men. Also he bade his comrades have a care of
his father and his son, and of the household
Gods, and girded him again with arms, and so
passed into the city. And first he went to the
wall, and to the gate by which he had come forth,
and then to his house, if haply she had returned

ÆNEAS AND THE SHADE OF CREÜSA

thither. But there indeed the men of Greece were come, and the fire had well-nigh mastered it. And after that he went to the citadel and to the palace of King Priam. And lo! in the porch of Juno's temple, Phœnix and Ulysses were keeping guard over the spoil, even the treasure of the temples, tables of the Gods, and solid cups of gold, and raiment, and a long array of them that had been taken captive, children and women. But not the less did he seek his wife through all the streets of the city, yea, and called her aloud by name. But lo! as he called, the image of her whom he sought seemed to stand before him, only greater than she had been while she was yet alive. And the spirit spake, saying, " Why art thou vainly troubled ? These things have not befallen us against the pleasure of the Gods. The ruler of Olympus willeth not that Creüsa should bear thee company in thy journey. For thou hast a long journey to take, and many seas to cross, till thou come to the Hesperian shore, where Lydian Tiber flows softly through a good land and a fertile. There shalt thou have great prosperity, and take to thyself a wife of royal race. Weep not then for Creüsa, whom thou lovest, nor think that I shall be carried away to be a bond-slave to some Grecian woman. Such fate befits not a daughter of Dardanus and daughter-in-law of Venus. The mighty Mother of the Gods keepeth me in this land to serve her. And now, farewell, and love the young Ascanius, even thy son and mine."

So spake the spirit, and, when Æneas wept and would have spoken, vanished out of his sight. Thrice he would have cast his arms about her neck, and thrice the image mocked him, being thin as air and fleeting as a dream. Then, the night being now spent, he sought his comrades, and found with much joy and wonder that a great company of men and women were gathered together, and were willing, all of them, to follow him whithersoever he went. And now the morning star rose over Mount Ida, and Æneas, seeing that the Greeks held the city, and that there was no longer any hope of succour, went his way to the mountains, taking with him his father.

CHAPTER IV.

Now for what remained of that year (for it was the time of summer when Troy was taken), Æneas, and they that were gathered to him, builded themselves ships for the voyage, dwelling the while under Mount Ida; and when the summer was well-nigh come again the work was finished, and the old man Anchises commanded that they should tarry no longer. Whereupon they sailed, taking also their Gods with them.

There was a certain land of Thrace, which the god Mars loved beyond all other lands, whereof in time past the fierce Lycurgus, who would have slain Bacchus, was king. Here, therefore, for the men of the land were friendly, or, at the least, had been before evil days came upon Troy, Æneas builded him a city, and called it after his own name. But, after awhile, as he did sacrifice on a certain day to his mother, even Venus, that he might have a blessing on his work, slaying also a white bull to Jupiter, there befell a certain horrible thing. For hard by the place where he did sacrifice there was a little hill, with much cornel and myrtle upon it, whereto Æneas coming would have plucked wands having leaves upon them, that he might cover therewith the altars. But lo! when he plucked a wand there dropped drops of blood therefrom. Whereupon great fear came on him, and wonder also. And when seeking to know the cause of the thing he plucked other wands also, there dropped blood even as before. Then, having prayed to the nymphs of the land and to Father Mars that they would turn all evil from him, he essayed the third time with all his might, setting his knee against the ground, to pluck forth a wand. Whereupon there issued from the hill a lamentable voice, saying, " Æneas, why doest thou me such cruel hurt, nor leavest me in peace in my grave ? For indeed I am no stranger to thee, nor strange is this blood which thou seest. Fly, for the land is cruel, and the shore greedy of gain.

I am Polydorus. Here was I pierced through with spears, which have grown into these wands that thou seest."

But Æneas when he heard the voice was sore dismayed, and he remembered him how King Priam, thinking that it might fare ill with him and the great city of Troy, had sent his son, Polydorus, by stealth, and much gold with him, to Polymestor, who was king of Thrace, and how the king, when Troy had now perished, slew the boy, and took the gold to himself. For of a truth the love of gold is the root of all evil. And Æneas told the thing to his father and to the chiefs ; and the sentence of all was that they should depart from the evil land. But first they made a great funeral for Polydorus, making a high mound of earth, and building thereon an altar to the dead. This also they bound about with garlands of sad - coloured wool and cypress, and the women of Troy stood about it with their hair loosened, as is the use of them that mourn. They offered also bowls of warm milk and blood, and laid the spirit in the tomb, bidding him farewell three times with a loud voice.

After this, when the time for voyaging was
come, and the south wind blew softly, they
launched the ships and set sail.   And first they
came to the island of Delos, which, having
been used to wander over the sea, the Lord
of the Silver Bow made fast, binding it to
Myconos and Gyaros, and found there quiet
anchorage.   And when they landed to worship,
there met them Anius, who was priest and king
of the place, having a crown of bay‑leaves
about his head, who knew Anchises for a friend
in time past, and used to them much hospitality.
Then did they pray to the god, saying, "Give
us, we beseech thee, a home where we may
dwell, and a name upon the earth, and a city
that shall abide, even a second Troy for them
that have escaped from the hands of Achilles
and the Greeks.   And do thou answer us, and
incline our hearts that we may know."

But when Æneas had ended these words,
straightway the place was shaken, even the
gates of the temple and the bay-trees that were
hard by.   And when they were all fallen to the
ground there came 'a voice, saying, "Son of
Dardanus, the land that first bare you shall

receive you again. Seek, then, your ancient
mother. Thence shall the children of Æneas
bear rule over all lands, yea, and their children's
children to many generations." Which when
they had heard, they greatly rejoiced, and would
fain know what was the city whither Phœbus
would have them go, that they might cease
from their wanderings. Then Anchises, ponder-
ing in his heart the things which he had learnt
from men of old time, spake thus : " There
lieth in mid-ocean a certain island of Crete,
wherein is a mountain, Ida. There was the
first beginning of our nation. Thence came
Teucer, our first father, to the land of Troy.
Let us go, then, whither the Gods would send
us, first doing sacrifice to the Winds ; and, indeed, if but Jupiter help us, 'tis but a three
days' journey for our ships."

So they offered sacrifice, a bull to Neptune
and a bull to the beautiful Apollo, and a black
sheep to the Storm and a white sheep to the
West Wind. There came also a rumour that
Idomeneus the Cretan had fled from his father's
kingdom, and that the land was ready for him
who should take it. Whereupon the men of

4

Troy set sail with a good heart, and passing among the islands that are called Cyclades, the wind blowing favourably behind them, so came to Crete. There they builded a city, and called its name Pergamea, after Pergama, which was the citadel of Troy. And for a while they tilled the soil; also they married and were given in marriage, as purposing to abide in the land. But there came a wasting sickness on the men, and a blight also on the trees and harvests, filling the year with death. The fields likewise were parched with drought, and the staff of bread was broken. Then the old Anchises bade them go yet again to the oracle at Delos, and inquire of the god what end there should be of these troubles, whence they should seek for help, and whither they should go.

But as Æneas slept there appeared to him the household Gods, which he had carried out of the burning of Troy, very clear to see in the light of the moon, which shone through the window of his chamber. And they spake unto him, saying, " Apollo bids us tell thee here that which he will tell thee if thou goest to Delos. We who have followed thee over many seas,

even we will bring thy children's children to
great honour, and make their city ruler over
many nations. Faint not, therefore, at thy long
wandering. Thou must seek yet another home.
For it was not in Crete that Apollo bade thee
dwell. There is a land which the Greeks call
Hesperia; an ancient land, whose inhabitants
are mighty men of valour; a land of vineyards
and wheat. There is our proper home, and
thence came Dardanus our father. Do thou,
therefore, tell these things to the old man
Anchises. Seek ye for the land of Hesperia,
which men also call Italy; but as for Crete,
Jupiter willeth not that ye should dwell there."

And for a while Æneas lay in great fear,
with a cold sweat upon him, so clear was the
vision of those whom he saw, nor in anywise
like unto a dream. Then he rose up from his
bed, and after prayer and sacrifice told the thing
to Anchises. And the old man saw that he
had been deceived in this matter, and he said,
"O my son, now do I remember how Cassandra was wont to prophesy these things to
me, and would speak of Hesperia and of the
land of Italy. But, indeed, no man thought in

those days that the men of Troy should voyage
to Hesperia; nor did any take account of the
words of Cassandra. But now let us heed the
oracle of Apollo, and depart."

So the men of Troy made their ships ready
and departed. And after a while, when they
could no more see the land, there fell a great
storm upon them, with a strong wind and great
rolling waves, and much lightning also. Thus
were they driven out of their course, and for
three days and nights saw neither the sun nor
the stars. But on the fourth day they came to
a land where they saw hills, and smoke rising
therefrom. Then did the men ply their oars
amain, and soon came to the shore. Now this
place they found to be one of certain islands
which men name the Strophades. And upon
these islands dwell creatures which are called
Harpies, very evil indeed, having the counte-
nances of women and wings like unto the wings
of birds and long claws. Also their faces are
pale as with much hunger. Now when the men
of Troy were come to this land, they saw many
herds of oxen and flocks of goats thereon, nor
any one to watch them. Of these they slew such

THE HARPIES

as they needed, and, not forgetting to give due share to the Gods, made a great feast upon the shore. But lo! even while they made merry, there came a great rushing of wings, and the Harpies came upon them, making great havoc of the meat and fouling all things most horribly. And when they had departed, the men of Troy sought another place where they might do sacrifice and eat their meat in peace. But when the Harpies had come thither also and done in the same fashion, Æneas commanded that the men should draw their swords and do battle with the beasts. Therefore, the Harpies coming yet again, Misenus with his trumpet gave the sound for battle. But lo! they fought as those that beat the air, seeing that neither sword nor spear availed to wound the beasts. Then again these departed, one only remaining, by name Celæno, who, sitting on a rock, spake after this fashion: "Do ye purpose, sons of Laomedon, to fight for these cattle that ye have wrongfully taken, or to drive the Harpies from their kingdom and inheritance? Hear, therefore, my words, which indeed the almighty Father told to Phœbus, and Phœbus told to me. Ye journey to Italy, and to Italy shall ye come. Only ye shall not build a city, and wall it about with walls, till dreadful hunger shall cause you to eat the very tables whereon ye sup."

So saying, she departed. But when great fear was fallen upon all, Anchises lifted up his hands to heaven and prayed to the Gods that they would keep that evil from them.

CHAPTER V.

THEN they set sail, and, the south wind blowing,
passed by Zacynthus and Dulichium, and also
Ithaca, which they cursed as they passed, because it was the land of the hateful Ulysses,
and so came to Actium, where they landed.
There also they did sacrifice to the Gods, and
had games of wrestling and others, rejoicing
that they had passed safely through so many
cities of their enemies. And there they wintered,
and Æneas fixed on the doors of the temple of
Apollo a shield of bronze which he had won in
battle from the valiant Abas, writing thereon
these words, "ÆNEAS DEDICATES THESE ARMS
WON FROM THE VICTORIOUS GREEKS."

But when the spring was come they set sail,
and, leaving behind them the land of Phæacia,
came to Buthrotum that is in Epirus. There
indeed they heard a marvellous thing, even that

Helenus, the son of Priam, was king in these parts, in the room of Pyrrhus, the son of Achilles, having also to wife Andromaché, who was the widow of Hector. And when Æneas, wishing to know whether these things were so, journeyed towards the city, lo! in a grove hard by, by a river which also was called Simoïs, there stood this same Andromaché, and made offerings to the spirit of Hector not without many tears. And at the first when she saw Æneas, and that he wore such arms as the men of Troy were used to wear, she swooned with fear, but after a while spake thus: "Is this indeed a real thing that I see? Art thou alive? or, if thou art dead, tell me, where is my Hector?" So she cried and wept aloud. And Æneas answered her: "Yes, lady, this is flesh and blood, and not a spirit, that thou seest. But as for thee, what fortune has befallen thee? Art thou still wedded to Pyrrhus?"

And she, casting down her eyes, made answer, "O daughter of Priam, happy beyond thy sisters in that thou wast slain at the tomb of Achilles, nor wast taken to be a prey of the conqueror! But as for me I was borne across the sea, to be

slave of the haughty son of Achilles. And
when he took to wife Hermione, who was the
daughter of Helen, he gave me to Helenus,
as a slave is given to a slave. But Pyrrhus,
after awhile, Orestes slew, taking him unawares,
even by the altar of his father. And when he
was dead, part of his kingdom came to Helenus,
who hath called the land Chaonia, after Chaon of
Troy ; and hath also builded a citadel, a new
Pergama, upon the hills. But tell me, was it
some storm that drave thee hither, or chance, or,
lastly, some sending of the Gods? And is Ascanius yet alive—the boy whom I remember ?
Does he yet think of his mother that is dead ?
And is he stout and of a good courage, as befits
the son of Æneas and sister's son to Hector ? "

And while she spake there came Helenus
from the city with a great company, and bade
welcome to his friends with much joy. And
Æneas saw how that all things were ordered
and named even as they had been at Troy,
only the things at Troy had been great, and
these were very small. And afterwards King
Helenus made a feast to them in his house,
and they drank together and were merry.

But after certain days were passed, Æneas,
seeing that the wind favoured them, spake to
Helenus, knowing him also to be a prophet of
the Gods: " Tell me now, seeing that thou art
wise in all manner of divination and prophecy,
how it will fare with us.   For indeed all things
have seemed to favour us, and we go not on
this journey against the will of the Gods, yet did
the Harpy Celæno prophesy evil things, that we
should endure great extremity of hunger.   Say,
then, of what things I should most beware, and
how I shall best prosper."

Then Helenus, after due sacrifice, led Æneas
to the temple of Phœbus.   And when they were
come thither, and the god had breathed into the
seer, even into Helenus, the spirit of prophecy,
he spake, saying, " Son of Venus, that thou
takest thy journey across the sea with favour
of the Gods, is manifest.   Hearken, therefore,
and I will inform thee of certain things, though
indeed they be few out of many, by which thou
mayest more safely cross unknown seas and get
thee to thy haven in Italy.   Much indeed the
Fates suffer me not to know, and much Juno
forbids me to speak.   Know then, first of all,

that Italy, which thou ignorantly thinkest to be
close at hand, is yet far away across many seas.
And let this be a sign to thee that thou art
indeed come to the place where thou wouldst
be.   When thou shalt see a white sow and
thirty pigs at her teats, then hast thou found
the place of thy city that shall be.   And as to
the devouring of thy tables for famine, heed it
not: Apollo will help thee at need.   But seek
not to find a dwelling - place on this shore of
Italy which is near at hand, seeing that it is
inhabited by the accursed sons of Greece.
And when thou hast passed it by, and art come
to the land of Sicily, and shalt see the strait of
Pelorus open before thee, do thou keep to thy
left hand and avoid the way that is on thy
right.   For here in days past was the land rent
asunder, so that the waters of the sea flow
between cities and fields that of old time were
joined together.   And on the right hand is
Scylla, and on the left Charybdis the whirlpool.
But Scylla dwelleth in her cave, a monster
dreadful to behold; for to the middle she is a fair
woman, but a beast of the sea below, even the
belly of a dolphin, with heads as of a wolf.

Wherefore it will be better for thee to fetch a compass round the whole land of Sicily than to come nigh these things, or to see them with thine eyes. Do thou also remember this, at all places and times, before all other Gods to worship Juno, that thou mayest persuade her, and so make thy way safely to Italy. And when thou art come thither, seek the Sibyl that dwelleth at Cumæ, the mad prophetess that writeth the sayings of Fate upon the leaves of a tree. For these indeed at the first abide in their places, but, the gate being opened, the wind blows them hither and thither. And when they are scattered she careth not to join them again, so that they who would inquire of her depart without an answer. Refuse not to tarry awhile, that thou mayest take counsel of her, though all things seem to prosper thy journey and thy comrades chide thy delay. For she shall tell thee all that shall befall thee in Italy — what wars thou shalt wage, and what perils thou must endure, and what avoid. So much, and no more, is it lawful for me to utter. Do thou depart, and magnify our country of Troy even to the heaven."

And when the seer had ended these sayings he commanded his people that they should carry to the ships gifts: gold, and carvings of ivory, and much silver, and caldrons that had been wrought at Dodona; also a coat of chain mail, and a helmet with a fair plume, which Pyrrhus had worn. Also he gave gifts to the old man Anchises. Horses, too, he gave, and guides for the journey, and tackling for the ships, and arms for the whole company. Then did he bid farewell to the old Anchises. Andromaché also came, bringing broidered robes, and for Ascanius a Phrygian cloak, and many like things, which she gave him, saying, " Take these works of my hands, that they may witness to thee of the abiding love of her that was once Hector's wife. For indeed thou art the very image of my Astyanax; so like are thy eyes and face and hands. And indeed he would now be of an age with thee." Then Æneas also said farewell, weeping the while. " Be ye happy, whose wanderings are over and rest already won; ye have no seas to cross, nor fields of Italy, still flying as we advance, to seek. Rather ye have the likeness of Troy before your eyes. And be sure that if ever I come to this land of Italy which I seek, there shall be friendship between you and me, and between your children and my children, for ever."

Then they set sail, and at eventide drew their ships to the land and slept on the beach. But at midnight Palinurus, the pilot, rising from his bed, took note of the winds and of the stars, even of Arcturus, and the Greater Bear and the Less, and Orion with his belt of gold. Seeing therefore that all things boded fair weather to come, he blew loud the signal that they should depart; which they did forthwith. And when the morning was now growing red in the east, behold a land with hills dimly seen and shores lying low in the sea. And, first of all, the old man Anchises cried, "Lo! there is Italy," and after him all the company. Then took Anchises a mighty cup, and filled it with wine, and, standing on the stern, said, "Gods of sea and land, and ye that have power of the air, give us an easy journey, and send such winds as may favour us." And even as he spake the wind blew more strongly behind. Also the harbour

mouth grew wider to behold, and on the hills
was seen a temple of Minerva. And lo! upon
the shore four horses white as snow, which the
old man seeing, said, " Thou speakest of war,
land of the stranger; for the horse signifieth
war, yet doth he also use himself to run in the
chariot, and to bear the bit in company; therefore also will we hope for peace." Then did they
sacrifice to Minerva, and to Juno also, which
rites the seer Helenus had chiefly commanded.
And this being done they trimmed their sails
and departed from the shore, fearing lest some
enemy, the Greeks being in that place, should
set upon them. So did they pass by Tarentum,
which Hercules builded, also the hills of
Caulon, and Scylacium, where many ships are
broken. And from Scylacium they beheld
Ætna, and heard a great roaring of the sea, and
saw also the waves rising up to heaven. Then
said Anchises, " Lo! this is that Charybdis
whereof the seer Helenus spake to us. Ply
your oars, my comrades, and let us fly therefrom." So they strove amain in rowing, and
Palinurus also steered to the left, all the other
ships following him. And many times the waves

lifted them to the heaven, and many times caused them to go down to the deep. But at the last, at setting of the sun, they came to the land of the Cyclops.

There, indeed, they lay in a harbour, well sheltered from all winds that blow, but all the night Ætna thundered dreadfully, sending forth a cloud with smoke of pitch, and ashes fiery hot, and also balls of fire, and rocks withal that had been melted with heat. For indeed men say that the giant Enceladus lieth under this mountain, being scorched with the lightning of Jupiter, and that from him cometh forth this flame; also that when, being weary, he turneth from one side to the other, the whole land of the Three Capes is shaken. All that night they lay in much fear, nor knew what the cause of this uproar might be, for indeed the sky was cloudy, nor could the moon be seen.

And when it was morning, lo! there came forth from the woods a stranger, very miserable to behold, in filthy garments fastened with thorns, and with beard unshaven, who stretched out to them his hands as one who prayed. And the men of Troy knew him to be a Greek. But he, seeing them, and knowing of what country they were, stood awhile in great fear, but afterwards ran very swiftly towards them, and used to them many prayers, weeping also the while. " I pray you, men of Troy, by the stars and by the Gods, and by this air which we breathe, to take me away from this land, whithersoever ye will. And indeed I ask not whither. That I am a Greek, I confess, and also that I bare arms against Troy. Wherefore drown me, if ye will, in the sea. For gladly will I die, if die I must, by the hands of men."

And he clung to their knees. Then Æneas bade him tell who he was, and how he came to be in this plight. And the man made answer, " I am a man of Ithaca, and a comrade of the unhappy Ulysses. My name is Achæmenides, and my father was Adamastus. And when my comrades fled from this accursed shore they left me in the Cyclops' cave. Hideous is he to see, and savage, and of exceeding great stature, and he feeds on the flesh of men. I myself saw with these eyes how he lay and caught two of my companions and brake them on the stone ; aye, and I saw their limbs quiver between his

5

teeth. Yet did he not do such things unpunished, for Ulysses endured not to behold
these deeds, and when the giant lay asleep,
being overcome with wine, we, after prayer made
to the Gods and lots cast what each should do,
bored out his eye, for one eye he had, huge as
a round shield of Argos, or as the circle of the
sun, and so did we avenge our comrades' death.
Do ye then fly with all the speed ye may. For
know that as this shepherd Polyphemus — a
shepherd he is by trade — so are a hundred
other Cyclopés, huge and savage as he, who
dwell on these shores and wander over the
hills. And now for three months have I dwelt
in these woods, eating berries and cornels and
herbs of the field. And when I saw your ships
I hastened to meet them. Do ye with me,
therefore, as ye will, so that I flee from this
accursed race."

And even while he spake the men of Troy saw
the shepherd Polyphemus among his flocks, and
that he made as if he would come to the shore.
Horrible to behold was he, huge and shapeless
and blind. And when he came to the sea he
washed the blood from the wound, grinding his

teeth the while, and though he went far into
the sea, yet did not the waves touch his middle.
And the men of Troy, having taken the suppliant on board, fled with all their might; and
he hearing their rowing would have reached to
them, but could not. Therefore did he shout
aloud, and the Cyclopés hearing him hasted to
the shore. Then did the men of Troy behold
them, a horrid company, tall as a grove of oaks
or cypresses. Nor knew they in their fear
what they should do, seeing that on the one
hand was the land of the Cyclopés, and on the
other Scylla and Charybdis, of which the seer
Helenus had bidden them beware. But while
they doubted, there blew a north wind from
Pelorus, wherewith they sailed onwards, and
Achæmenides with them. So they came to
Ortygia, whither, as men say, the river Alpheüs
floweth under the sea from the land of Pelops,
and so mingleth with Arethusa; and afterwards
they passed the promontory of Pachynus, Ca-
marina also, and Gela, and other cities likewise, till they came to Lilybæum, and so at last
to Drepanum. There the old man Anchises died,
and was buried.

CHAPTER VI.

THE SHIPWRECK.

Not many days after Æneas and his companions set sail. But scarce were they out of sight of the land of Sicily when Juno espied them. Very wroth was she that they should be now drawing near to the end of their journey, and she said to herself, "Shall I be baulked of my purpose, nor be able to keep these men of Troy from Italy? Minerva, indeed, because one man sinned, even Ajax Oïleus, burned the fleet of the Greeks, and drowned the men in the sea. For the ships she smote with the thunderbolts of Jupiter; and as for Ajax, him she caught up with a whirlwind, and dashed him upon the rocks, piercing him through. Only I, though I be both sister and wife to Jupiter, avail nothing against this people. And who that heareth this in after time shall pay me due honour and sacrifice?"

Then she went, thinking these things in her heart, to the land of Æolia, where King Æolus keepeth the winds under bolt and bar. Mightily do they roar within the mountain, but their king restraineth them and keepeth them in bounds, being indeed set to do this very thing, lest they should carry both the heavens and the earth before them in their great fury. To him said Juno, " O Æolus, whom Jupiter hath made king of the winds, a nation which I hate is sailing over the Tuscan sea. Loose now thy storms against them, and drown their ships in the sea. And hearken what I will do for thee. Twelve maidens I have that wait on me continually, who are passing fair, and the fairest of all, even Deiopëia, I will give thee to wife."

To whom answered King Æolus, " It is for thee, O Queen, to order what thou wilt, it being of thy gift that I hold this sovereignty and eat at the table of the Gods."

So saying he drave in with his spear the folding-doors of the prison of the winds, and these straightway in a great host rushed forth, even all the winds together, and rolled great waves upon the shore. And straightway there arose a great shouting of men and straining of cables; nor could the sky nor the light of the day be seen any more, but a darkness as of night came down upon the sea, and there were thunders and lightnings over the whole heavens.

Then did Æneas grow cold with fear, and stretching out his hands to heaven he cried, "Happy they who fell under the walls of Troy, before their fathers' eyes! Would to the Gods that thou hadst slain me, Diomed, bravest of the Greeks, even as Hector fell by the spear of Achilles, or tall Sarpedon, or all the brave warriors whose dead bodies Simoïs rolled down to the sea!"

But as he spake a blast of wind struck his sails from before, and his ship was turned broadside to the waves. Three others also were tossed upon the rocks which men call the "Altars," and three into the quicksands of the Syrtis. And another, in which sailed the men of Lycia, with Orontes, their chief, was struck upon the stern by a great sea and sunk. And when Æneas looked, lo! there were some swimming in the waves, and broken planks also, and arms and treasures of Troy. Others also were

shattered by the waves, as those of Ilioneus and
Achates, and of Abas and the old man Alethes.

But King Neptune was aware of the tumult
where he sat at the bottom of the sea, and rais-
ing his head above the waves, looked forth and
saw how the ships were scattered abroad and
the men of Troy were in sore peril. Also he
knew his sister's wrath and her craft. Then he
called to him the winds and said, " What is this,
ye winds, that ye trouble heaven and earth without leave of me ? Now will I—but I must first
bid the waves be still, only be sure that ye shall
not thus escape hereafter. Begone, and tell your
king that the dominion over the sea belongeth
unto me, and bid him keep him to his rocks."

Then he bade the waves be still; also he
scattered the clouds and brought back the sun.
And Cymothea and Triton, gods of the sea, drew
the ships from the rocks, Neptune also lifting
them with his trident. Likewise he opened the
quicksands, and delivered the ships that were
therein. And this being done he crossed the
sea in his chariot, and the waves beholding him
sank to rest, even as it befalls when there is
sedition in the city, and the people are wroth,

and men throw stones and firebrands, till lo! of a sudden there cometh forth a reverend sire, a good man and true, and all men are silent and hearken to him ; and the uproar is stayed. So was the sea stilled, beholding its king.

Then Æneas and his companions, being sore wearied with the storm, made for the nearest shore, even Africa, where they found a haven running far into the land, into which the waves come not till their force be spent. On either side thereof are cliffs very high, and shining woods over them. Also at the harbour's head is a cave and a spring of sweet water within, a dwelling-place of the Nymphs. Hither came Æneas, with seven ships. Right glad were the men of Troy to stand upon the dry land again. Then Achates struck a spark out of flint, and they lighted a fire with leaves and the like ; also they took of the wheat which had been in the ships, and made ready to parch and to bruise it, that they might eat. Meanwhile Æneas had climbed the cliff, if haply he might see some of his companions' ships. These indeed he saw not, but he espied three great stags upon the shore and a herd following them.

NEPTUNE STILLING THE WAVES.

Wherefore, taking the arrows and the bow
which Achates bare with him, he let fly, slaying
the leaders and others also, till he had gotten
seven, one for each ship. Then made he his
way to the landing-place, and divided the prey.
Also he made distribution of the wine which
Acestes, their host in Sicily, had given them as
they were about to depart, and spake comfort-
able words to them, saying, "O my friends,
be ye sure that there will be an end to these
troubles ; and indeed ye have suffered worse
things before. Be ye of good cheer therefore.
Haply ye shall one day have pleasure in thinking of these things. For be sure that the Gods
have prepared a dwelling-place for us in Italy,
where we shall build a new Troy, in great peace
and happiness. Wherefore endure unto the
day of prosperity."

Then they made ready the feast, and roasted
of the meat upon spits, and boiled other in
water. Also they drank of the wine and were
comforted. And after supper they talked much
of them that were absent, doubting whether
they were alive or dead.

CHAPTER VII.

ALL these things did Jupiter behold ; and even
as he beheld them there came to him Venus,
having a sad countenance and her shining eyes
dim with tears, and spake: " O great Father, that
rulest all things, what have Æneas and the men
of Troy sinned against thee, that the whole world
is shut against them ?   Didst not thou promise
that they should rule over land and sea ? Why,
then, art thou turned back from thy purpose ?
With this I was wont to comfort myself for the
evil fate of Troy, but lo ! this same fate follows
them still, nor is there any end to their troubles.
And yet it was granted to Antenor, himself
also a man of Troy, that he should escape from
the Greeks, and coming to the Liburnian land,
where Timavus flows with much noise into the
sea, build a city and find rest for himself.   But
we, who are thy children, are kept far from the
land which thou hast sworn to give us."

Then her father kissed her once and again,
and answered smiling, " Fear not, my daughter,
the fate of thy children changeth not. Thou
shalt see this city for which thou lookest, and
shalt receive thy son, the great-hearted Æneas,
into the heavens. Hearken, therefore, and I will
tell thee things to come. Æneas shall war with
the nations of Italy, and shall subdue them, and
build a city, and rule therein for three years.
And after the space of thirty years shall the boy
Ascanius, who shall hereafter be called Iülus
also, change the place of his throne from Lavinium unto Alba ; and for three hundred years
shall there be kings in Alba of the kindred of
Hector. Then shall a priestess bear to Mars
twin sons, whom a she-wolf shall suckle ; of
whom the one, even Romulus, shall build a
city, dedicating it to Mars, and call it Rome,
after his own name. To which city have I
given empire without bound or end. And
Juno also shall repent her of her wrath, and
join counsel with me, cherishing the men of
Rome, so that they shall bear rule even over
Argos and Mycenæ."

And when he had said this, he sent down his

messenger, even Mercury, to turn the heart of Dido and her people, where they dwelt in the city of Carthage, which they had builded, so that they should deal kindly with the strangers.

Now it came to pass on the next day that Æneas, having first hidden his ships in a bay that was well covered with trees, went forth to spy out the new land whither he was come, and Achates only went with him. And Æneas had in each hand a broad-pointed spear. And as he went there met him in the middle of the wood his mother, but habited as a Spartan virgin, for she had hung a bow from her shoulders after the fashion of a huntress, and her hair was loose, and her tunic short to the knees, and her garments gathered in a knot upon her breast. Then first the false huntress spake, " If perchance ye have seen one of my sisters wandering hereabouts, make known to me the place. She is girded with a quiver, and is clothed with the skin of a spotted lynx, or, may be, she hunts a wild boar with horn and hound."

To whom Æneas, " I have not seen nor heard sister of thine, O virgin—for what shall I call thee ? for, of a surety, neither is thy look as of a mortal woman, nor yet thy voice. A goddess certainly thou art, sister of Phœbus, or, haply, one of the nymphs. But whosoever thou art, look favourably upon us and help us. Tell us in what land we be, for the winds have driven us hither, and we know not aught of place or people."

And Venus said, "Nay, stranger I am not such as ye think. We virgins of Tyre are wont to carry a quiver and to wear a buskin of purple. For indeed it is a Tyrian city that is hard by, though the land be Lybia. And of this city Dido is queen, having come hither from Tyre, flying from the wrongdoing of her brother. And indeed the story of the thing is long, but I will recount the chief matter thereof to thee. The husband of this Dido was one Sichæus, richest among all the men of Phœnicia, and greatly beloved of his wife, whom he married from a virgin. Now the brother of this Sichæus was Pygmalion, the king of the country, and he exceeded all men in wickedness. And when there arose a quarrel between them, the king, being exceedingly mad after gold, took him unaware, even as he did sacrifice at the altar, and slew him. And the king hid the matter many days from Dido, and cheated her with false hopes. But at the last there came to her in her dreams the likeness of the dead man, baring his wounds and showing the wickedness which had been done. Also he bade her make haste and fly from that land, and, that she might do this the more easily, told her of great treasure, gold and silver, that was hidden in the earth. And Dido, being much moved by these things, made ready for flight; also she sought for companions, and there came together to her all as many as hated the king or feared him. Then did they seize ships that chanced to be ready, and laded them with gold, even the treasure of King Pygmalion, and so fled across the sea. And in all this was a woman the leader. Then came they to this place, where thou seest the walls and citadel of Carthage, and bought so much land as they could cover with a bull's hide. And now do ye answer me this, Whence come ye, and whither do ye go?"

Then answered Æneas, "Should I tell the whole story of our wanderings, and thou have leisure to hear, evening would come ere I could

make an end. We are men of Troy, who, having journeyed over many seas, have now been
driven by storms to this shore of Lybia. And
as for me, men call me the prince Æneas. The
land I seek is Italy, and my race is from Jupiter
himself. With twenty ships did I set sail, going
in the way whereon the Gods sent me. And of
these scarce seven are left. And now, seeing
that Europe and Asia endure me not, I wander
over the desert places of Africa."

But Venus suffered him not to speak more,
but said, " Whoever thou art, stranger, that art
come to this Tyrian city, thou art surely beloved
by the Gods. And now go, show thyself to
the queen. And as for thy ships and thy companions, I tell that they are safe in the haven,
if I have not learnt augury in vain. See those
twenty swans, how joyously they fly ! And now
there cometh an eagle swooping down from
the sky, putting them to confusion, but now
again they move in due order, and some are
settling on the earth and some preparing to
settle. Even so doth it fare with thy ships, for
either are they already in the haven or enter
thereinto with sails full set."

And as she spake she turned away, and there shone a rosy light from her neck, also there came from her hair a sweet savour as of ambrosia, and her garments grew unto her feet; and Æneas perceived that she was his mother, and cried aloud,—

"O my mother, why dost thou mock me so often with false shows, nor sufferest me to join my hand unto thy hand, and to speak with thee face to face?"

And he went towards the walls of the city. But Venus covered him and his companions with a mist, that no man might see them, or hinder them, or inquire of their business, and then departed to Paphos, where was her temple and also many altars of incense. Then the men hastened on their way, and mounting a hill which hung over the city, marvelled to behold it, for indeed it was very great and noble, with mighty gates and streets, and a multitude that walked therein. For some built the walls and the citadel, rolling great stones with their hands, and others marked out places for houses. Also they chose those that should give judgment and bear rule in the city. Some, too, digged out

harbours, and others laid the foundations of a
theatre, and cut out great pillars of stone. Like
to bees they were, when, the summer being newly
come, the young swarms go forth, or when they
labour filling the cells with honey, and some
receive the burdens of those that return from the
fields, and others keep off the drones from the
hive. Even so laboured the men of Tyre. And
when Æneas beheld them he cried, " Happy ye,
who even now have a city to dwell in!" And
being yet hidden with the mist, he went in at
the gate and mingled with the men, being seen
of none.

Now in the midst of the city was a wood, very
thick with trees, and here the men of Carthage,
first coming to the land from their voyage, had
digged out of the ground that which Juno had
said should be a sign to them, even a horse's
head ; for that, finding this, their city would be
mighty in war, and full of riches. Here, then,
Dido was building a temple to Juno, very splendid, with threshold of bronze, and many steps
thereunto ; of bronze also were the door-posts
and the gates. And here befell a thing which
gave much comfort and courage to Æneas ; for

as he stood and regarded the place, waiting also
for the queen, he saw set forth in order upon
the walls the battles that had been fought at
Troy, the sons of Atreus also, and King Priam,
and fierce Achilles.   Then said he, not without
tears, " Is there any land, O Achates, that is not
filled with our sorrows?   Seest thou Priam?
Yet withal there is a reward for virtue here
also, and tears and pity for the troubles of men.
Fear not, therefore.   Surely the fame of these
things shall profit us."

Then he looked, satisfying his soul with the
paintings on the walls.   For there was the
city of Troy.   In this part of the field the
Greeks fled and the youth of Troy pursued
them, and in that the men of Troy fled, and
Achilles followed hard upon them in his chariot.
Also he saw the white tents of Rhesus, King of
Thrace, whom the fierce Diomed slew in his
sleep, when he was newly come to Troy, and
drave his horses to the camp before they ate of
the grass of the fields of Troy or drank the waters
of Xanthus.   There also Troïlus was pictured,
ill-matched in battle with the great Achilles.
His horses bare him along; but he lay on his

back in the chariot, yet holding the reins, and
his neck and head were dragged upon the earth,
and the spear-point made a trail in the dust.
And in another place the women of Troy went
suppliant-wise to the temple of Minerva, bearing
a great and beautiful robe, sad and beating their
breasts, and with hair unbound; but the goddess
regarded them not. Also Achilles dragged the
body of Hector three times round the walls of
Troy, and was selling it for gold. And Æneas
groaned when he saw the man whom he loved,
and the old man Priam reaching out helpless
hands. Also he knew himself, fighting in the
midst of the Grecian chiefs; black Memnon
also he knew, and the hosts of the East; and
Penthesilea leading the army of the Amazons,
with shields shaped as the moon. Fierce she
was to see, with one breast bared for battle, and
a golden girdle beneath it, a damsel daring to
fight with men.

CHAPTER VIII.

DIDO.

BUT while Æneas marvelled to see these things lo! there came, with a great throng of youths behind her, Dido, most beautiful of women, fair as Diana, when, on the banks of Eurotas or on the hills of Cynthus, she leads the dance with a thousand nymphs of the mountains about her. On her shoulder she bears a quiver, and over-tops them all, and her mother, even Latona, silently rejoices to behold her. So fair and seemly to see was Dido as she bare herself right nobly in the midst, being busy in the work of her kingdom. Then she sat herself down on a lofty throne in the gate of the temple, with many armèd men about her. And she did justice between man and man; also she divided the work of the city, sharing it equally or parting it by lot.

Then of a sudden Æneas heard a great

clamour, and saw a company of men come quickly to the place, among whom were Antheus and Sergestus and Cloanthus, and others of the men of Troy that had been parted from him in the storm. Right glad was he to behold them, yet was not without fear ; and though he would fain have come forth and caught them by the hand, yet did he tarry, waiting to hear how the men had fared, where they had left their ships, and wherefore they were come.

Then Ilioneus, leave being now given that he should speak, thus began : " O Queen, whom Jupiter permits to build a new city in these lands, we men of Troy, whom the winds have carried over many seas, pray thee that thou save our ships from fire, and spare a people that serveth the Gods. For, indeed, we are not come to waste the dwellings of this land, or to carry off spoils to our ships. For, of a truth, they who have suffered so much think not of such deeds. There is a land which the Greeks call Hesperia, but the people themselves Italy, after the name of their chief ; an ancient land, mighty in arms and fertile of corn. Hither were we journeying, when a storm arising scattered our ships, and only these few that thou seest escaped to the land. And can there be nation so savage that it receiveth not ship-wrecked men on its shore, but beareth arms against them, and forbiddeth them to land? Nay, but if ye care not for men, yet regard the Gods, who forget neither them that do right-eously nor them that transgress. We had a king, Æneas, than whom there lived not a man more dutiful to Gods and men, and greater in war. If indeed he be yet alive, then we fear not at all. For of a truth it will not repent thee to have helped us. And if not, other friends have we, as Acestes of Sicily. Grant us, therefore, to shelter our ships from the wind; also to fit them with fresh timber from the woods, and to make ready oars for rowing, so that, find-ing again our king and our companions, we may gain the land of Italy. But if he be dead, and Ascanius his son lost also, then there is a dwell-ing ready for us in the land of Sicily, with Acestes, who is our friend."

Then Dido, her eyes bent on the ground, thus spake, "Fear not, men of Troy. If we have seemed to deal harshly with you, pardon us, seeing that, being newly settled in this land, we must keep watch and ward over our coasts. But as for the men of Troy, and their deeds in arms, who knows them not ? Think not that we in Carthage are so dull of heart, or dwell so remote from man, that we are ignorant of these things. Whether, therefore, ye will journey to Italy, or rather return to Sicily and King Acestes, know that I will give you all help, and protect you; or, if ye will, settle in this land of ours. Yours is this city which I am building. I will make no difference between man of Troy and man of Tyre. Would that your king also were here ! Surely I will send those that shall seek him in all parts of Libya, lest haply he should be gone astray in any forest or strange city of the land."

And when Æneas and Achates heard these things they were glad, and would have come forth from the cloud, and Achates said, " What thinkest thou ? Lo, thy comrades are safe, saving him whom we saw with our own eyes drowned in the waves; and all other things are according as thy mother said."

And even as he spake the cloud parted from about them, and Æneas stood forth, very bright to behold, with face and breast as of a god, for his mother had given to him hair beautiful to see, and cast about him the purple light of youth, even as a workman sets ivory in some fair ornament, or compasseth about silver or marble of Paros with gold. Then spake he to the queen, "Lo! I am he whom ye seek, even Æneas of Troy, scarcely saved from the waters of the sea. And as for thee, O Queen, seeing that thou only hast been found to pity the unspeakable sorrows of Troy, and biddest us, though we be but poor exiles and lacking all things, to share thy city and thy home, may the Gods do so to thee as thou deservest. And, of a truth, so long as the rivers run to the seas, and the shadows fall on the hollows of the hills, so long will thy name and thy glory survive, whatever be the land to which the Gods shall bring me." Then gave he his right hand to Ilioneus, and his left hand to Sergestus, and greeted them with great joy.

And Dido, hearing these things, was silent for a while, but at the last she spake : "What ill fortune brings thee into perils so great? what power drave thee to these savage shores?

Well do I mind me how in days gone by there came to Sidon one Teucer, who, having been banished from his country, sought help from Belus that he might find a kingdom for himself. And it chanced that in those days Belus, my father, had newly conquered the land of Cyprus. From that day did I know the tale of Troy, and thy name also, and the chiefs of Greece. Also I remember that Teucer spake honourably of the men of Troy, saying that he was himself sprung of the old Teucrian stock. Come ye, therefore, to my palace. I too have wandered far, even as you, and so have come to this land, and having suffered much have learnt to succour them that suffer."

So saying she led Æneas into her palace; also she sent to his companions in the ships great store of provisions, even twenty oxen and a hundred bristly swine and a hundred ewe sheep with their lambs. But in the palace a great feast was set forth, couches covered with broidered purple, and silver vessels without end, and cups of gold, whereon were embossed the mighty deeds of the men of old time.

And in the mean time Æneas sent Achates in

haste to the ships, that he might fetch Ascanius
to the feast.   Also he bade that the boy should
bring with him gifts of such things as they had
saved from the ruins of Troy, a mantle stiff with
broidery of gold and a veil bordered with yellow
acanthus, which the fair Helen had taken with
her, flying from her home; but Leda, her mother,
had given them to Helen ; a sceptre likewise
which Ilione, first-born of the daughters of Priam,
had carried, and a necklace of pearls and a
double crown of jewels and gold.

But Venus was troubled in heart, fearing
evil to her son should the men of Tyre be
treacherous, after their wont, and Juno remember her wrath.   Wherefore, taking counsel with
herself, she called to the winged boy, even
Love, that was her son, and spake, " My son,
who art all my power and strength, who
laughest at the thunders of Jupiter, thou
knowest how Juno, being exceedingly wroth
against thy brother Æneas, causeth him to
wander out of the way over all lands.   This
day Dido hath him in her palace, and speaketh
him fair ; but I fear me much how these things
may end.   Wherefore hear thou that which I

purpose. Thy brother hath even now sent for the
boy Ascanius, that he may come to the palace,
bringing with him gifts of such things as they
saved from the ruins of Troy. Him will I
cause to fall into a deep sleep, and hide in
Cythera or Idalium, and do thou for one night
take upon thee his likeness. And when Queen
Dido at the feast shall hold thee in her lap, and
kiss and embrace thee, do thou breathe by
stealth thy fire into her heart."

Then did Love as his mother bade him,
and put off his wings, and took upon him the
shape of Ascanius, but on the boy Venus caused
there to fall a deep sleep, and carried him to
the woods of Idalium, and lapped him in sweet-
smelling flowers. And in his stead Love carried the gifts to the queen. And when he was
come they sat down to the feast, the queen
being in the midst under a canopy. Æneas
also and the men of Troy lay on coverlets of
purple, to whom serving-men brought water
and bread in baskets and napkins; and within
fifty handmaids were ready to replenish the
store of victual and to fan the fire ; and a hundred
others, with pages as many, loaded the tables

with dishes and drinking-cups. Many men of Tyre also were bidden to the feast. Much they marvelled at the gifts of Æneas, and much at the false Ascanius. Dido also could not satisfy herself with looking on him, nor knew what trouble he was preparing for her in the time to come. And he, having first embraced the father who was not his father, and clung about his neck, addressed himself to Queen Dido, and she ever followed him with her eyes, and sometimes would hold him on her lap. And still he worked upon her that she should forget the dead Sichæus and conceive a new love in her heart.

But when they first paused from the feast, lo! men set great bowls upon the table and filled them to the brim with wine. Then did the queen call for a great vessel of gold, with many jewels upon it, from which Belus, and all the kings from Belus, had drunk, and called for wine, and having filled it she cried, "O Jupiter, whom they call the god of hosts and guests, cause that this be a day of joy for the men of Troy and for them of Tyre, and that our children remember it for ever. Also, Bacchus, giver of joy, be present, and kindly Juno."

DIDO AND THE FALSE ASCANIUS

And when she had touched the wine with her
lips, she handed the great cup to Prince Bitias,
who drank thereout a mighty draught, and the
other princes after him. Then the minstrel
Iopas, whom Atlas himself had taught, sang to
the harp, of the moon, how she goes on her
way, and of the sun, how his light is darkened.
He sang also of men, and of the beasts of the
field, whence they come; and of the stars,
Arcturus, and the Greater Bear and the Less,
and the Hyades; and of the winter sun, why he
hastens to dip himself in the ocean; and of the
winter nights, why they tarry so long. The
queen also talked much of the story of Troy, of
Priam, and of Hector, asking many things, as
of the arms of Memnon, and of the horses of
Diomed, and of Achilles, how great he was.
And at last she said to Æneas, "Tell us now
thy story, how Troy was taken, and thy wanderings over land and sea." And Æneas made
answer, " Nay, O Queen, but thou biddest me
renew a sorrow unspeakable. Yet, if thou art
minded to hear these things, hearken." And
he told her all that had befallen him, even to
the day when his father Anchises died.

CHAPTER IX.

THE LOVE AND DEATH OF DIDO.

Much was Queen Dido moved by the story, and much did she marvel at him that told it, and scarce could sleep for thinking of him. And the next day she spake to Anna, her sister, "O my sister, I have been troubled this night with ill dreams, and my heart is disquieted within me. What a man is this stranger that hath come to our shores! How noble of mien! How bold in war! Sure I am that he is of the sons of the Gods. What fortunes have been his! Of what wars he told us! Surely were I not stead-fastly purposed that I would not yoke me again in marriage, this were the man to whom I might yield. Only he—for I will tell thee the truth, my sister—only he, since the day when Sichæus died by his brother's hand, hath moved my heart. But may the earth swallow me up, or the almighty Father strike me with lightning, ere I stoop to such baseness. The husband of my youth hath carried with him my love, and he shall keep it in his grave."

So she spake, with many tears. And her sister made answer, " Why wilt thou waste thy youth in sorrow, without child or husband ? Thinkest thou that there is care or remembrance of such things in the grave ? No suitors indeed have pleased thee here or in Tyre, but wilt thou also contend with a love that is after thine own heart ? Think too of the nations among whom thou dwellest, how fierce they are, and of thy brother at Tyre, what he threatens against thee. Surely it was by the will of the Gods, and of Juno chiefly, that the ships of Troy came hither. And this city, which thou buildest, to what greatness will it grow if only thou wilt make for thyself such alliance! How great will be the glory of Carthage if the strength of Troy be joined unto her! Only do thou pray to the Gods and offer sacrifices ; and, for the present, seeing that the time of sailing is now past, make excuse that these strangers tarry with thee awhile."

Thus did Anna comfort her sister and encourage her. And first the two offered sacrifice to the Gods, chiefly to Juno, who careth for the bond of marriage. Also, examining the entrails of slain beasts, they sought to learn the things that should happen thereafter. And ever Dido would company with Æneas, leading him about the walls of the city which she builded. And often she would begin to speak and stay in the midst of her words. And when even was come, she would hear again and again at the banquet the tale of Troy, and while others slept would watch, and while he was far away would seem to see him and to hear him. Ascanius, too, she would embrace for love of his father, if so she might cheat her own heart. But the work of the city was stayed meanwhile; nor did the towers rise in their places, nor the youth practise themselves in arms.

Then Juno, seeing how it fared with the queen, spake to Venus, "Are ye satisfied with your victory, thou and thy son, that ye have vanquished the two of you one woman? Well I knew that thou fearedst lest this Carthage should harm thy favourite. But why should there be war between us? Thou hast what

thou seekedst. Let us make alliance. Let Dido
obey a Phrygian husband, and bring the men
of Tyre as her dowry."

But Venus knew that she spake with ill intent,
to the end that the men of Troy should not
reign in the land of Italy. Nevertheless she
dissembled with her tongue, and spake, "Who
would not rather have peace with thee than
war? Only I doubt whether this thing shall be
to the pleasure of Jupiter. This thou must
learn, seeing that thou art his wife, and where
thou leadest I will follow."

So the two, taking counsel together, ordered
things in this wise. The next day a great
hunting was prepared. For as soon as ever
the sun was risen upon the earth, the youth of
the city assembled, with nets and hunting spears
and dogs that ran by scent. And the princes
of Carthage waited for the queen at the palace
door, where her horse stood champing the bit,
with trappings of purple and gold. And after
a while she came forth, with many following
her. And she had upon her a Sidonian mantle,
with a border wrought with divers colours ; of
gold was her quiver, and of gold the knot of

7

her hair, and of gold the clasp to her mantle.
Æneas likewise came forth, beautiful as is
Apollo when he leaveth Lydia and the stream
of Xanthus, coming to Delos, and hath about
his hair a wreath of bay-leaves and a circlet of
gold. So fair was Æneas to see. And when
the hunters came to the hills they found great
store of goats and stags, which they chased.
And of all the company Ascanius was the foremost, thinking scorn of such hunting, and wishing that a wild boar or a lion out of the hills
should come forth to be his prey.

And now befell a great storm, with much
thunder and hail, from which the hunters
sought shelter. But Æneas and the queen,
being left of all their company, came together
to the same cave. And there they plighted
their troth one to another. Nor did the queen
after that make secret of her love, but called
Æneas her husband.

Straightway went Rumour and told these
things through the cities of Libya. Now
Rumour, men say, is the youngest daughter of
Earth, a marvellous creature, moving very
swiftly with feet and wings, and having many

feathers upon her, and under every feather an eye and a tongue and a mouth and an ear. In the night she flies between heaven and earth, and sleepeth not; and in the day she sits on some housetop or lofty tower, or spreads fear over mighty cities; and she loveth that which is false even as she loveth that which is true. So now she went telling through Libya how Æneas of Troy was come, and Dido was wedded to him, and how they lived careless and at ease, and thinking not of the work to which they were called.

And first of all she went to Prince Iarbas, who himself had sought Dido in marriage. And Iarbas was very wroth when he heard it, and, coming to the temple of Jupiter, spread his grief before the god, how that he had given a place on his coasts to this Dido, and would have taken her to wife, but that she had married a stranger from Phrygia, another Paris, whose dress and adornments were of a woman rather than of a man.

And Jupiter saw that this was so, and he said to Mercury, who was his messenger, "Go speak to Æneas these words: 'Thus saith the

King of Gods and men. Is this what thy
mother promised of thee, twice saving thee
from the spear of the Greeks? Art thou he
that shall rule Italy and its mighty men of war,
and spread thy dominion to the ends of the
world? If thou thyself forgettest these things,
dost thou grudge to thy son the citadels of
Rome? What doest thou here? Why lookest
thou not to Italy? Depart and tarry not.'"

Then Mercury fitted the winged sandals to
his feet, and took the wand with which he
driveth the spirits of the dead, and came right
soon to Mount Atlas, which standeth bearing
the heaven on his head, and having always clouds
about his top, and snow upon his shoulders,
and a beard that is stiff with ice. There Mercury stood áwhile ; then, as a bird which seeks
its prey in the sea, shot headlong down, and
came to Æneas where he stood, with a yellow
jasper in his sword-hilt, and a cloak of purple
shot with gold about his shoulders, and spake:
" Buildest thou Carthage, forgetting thine own
work? The almighty Father saith to thee,
'What meanest thou? Why tarriest thou
here? If thou carest not for thyself, yet think

of thy son, and that the Fates have given to him Italy and Rome.' "

And Æneas saw him no more. And he stood stricken with fear and doubt. Fain would he obey the voice, and go as the Gods commanded. But how should he tell this purpose to the queen ? But at the last it seemed good to him to call certain of the chiefs, as Mnestheus, and Sergestus, and Antheus, and bid them make ready the ships in silence, and gather together the people, but dissemble the cause, and he himself would watch a fitting time to speak and unfold the matter to the queen.

Yet was not Dido deceived, for love is keen of sight. Rumour also told her that they made ready the ships for sailing. Then, flying through the city, even as one on whom has come the frenzy of Bacchus flies by night over Mount Cithæron, she came upon Æneas, and spake : " Thoughtest thou to hide thy crime, and to depart in silence from this land ? Carest thou not for her whom thou leavest to die ? And hast thou no fear of winter storms that vex the sea ? By all that I have done for thee and given thee, if there be yet any place for repent-

ance, repent thee of this purpose. For thy sake
I suffer the wrath of the princes of Libya and
of my own people; and if thou leavest me, for
what should I live?—till my brother overthrow
my city, or Iarbas carry me away captive? If
but I had a little Æneas to play in my halls
I should not seem so altogether desolate."

But Æneas, fearing the words of Jupiter,
stood with eyes that relented not. At the last
he spake: "I deny not, O Queen, the benefits
that thou hast done unto me, nor ever, while
I live, shall I forget Dido. I sought not to fly
by stealth; yet did I never promise that I
would abide in this place. Could I have chosen
according to my will I had built again the city
of Troy where it stood; but the Gods command
that I should seek Italy. Thou hast thy
Carthage: why dost thou grudge Italy to us?
Nor may I tarry. Night after night have I
seen my father Anchises warning me in dreams.
Also even now the messenger of Jupiter came
to me—with these ears I heard him—and bade
me depart."

Then, in great wrath, with eyes askance, did
Dido break forth upon him: "Surely no god-

dess was thy mother, nor art thou come of the
race of Dardanus. The rocks of Caucasus
brought thee forth, and an Hyrcanian tigress gave
thee suck. For why should I dissemble ? Was
he moved at all my tears ? Did he pity my love ?
Nay, the very Gods are against me. This man
I took to myself when he was shipwrecked and
ready to perish. I brought back his ships, his
companions from destruction. And now forsooth comes the messenger of Jupiter with
dreadful commands from the Gods. As for thee,
I keep thee not. Go, seek thy Italy across the
seas : only, if there is any vengeance in heaven,
thou wilt pay the penalty for this wrong, being
wrecked on some rock in their midst. Then
wilt thou call on Dido in vain. Aye, and wher-
ever thou shalt go I will haunt thee, and rejoice
in the dwellings below to hear thy doom."

Then she turned, and hasted to go into the
house. But her spirit left her, so that her
maidens bare her to her chamber and laid her
on her bed.

Then Æneas, though indeed he was much
troubled in heart, and would fain have comforted the queen, was obedient to the heavenly

word, and departed to his ships. And the men
of Troy busied themselves in making them
ready for the voyage. Even as the ants spoil a
great heap of corn and store it in their dwellings
against winter, moving in a black line across the
field, and some carry the great grains, and some
chide those that linger, even so did the Trojans
swarm along the ways and labour at the
work.

But when Dido saw it she called to Anna,
her sister, and said, "Seest thou how they
hasten the work along the shore? Even now
the sails are ready for the winds, and the
sailors have wreathed the ships with garlands,
as if for departure. Go thou — the deceiver
always trusted thee, and thou knowest how
best to move him — go and entreat him. I
harmed not him nor his people; let him then
grant me this only. Let him wait for a fairer
time for his journey. I ask not that he give up
his purpose; only that he grant me a short
breathing space, till I may learn how to bear this
sorrow."

And Anna hearkened to her sister, and took
the message to Æneas, yet profited nothing, for

the Gods shut his ears that he should not hear.
Even as an oak stands firm when the north wind
would root it up from the earth—its leaves are
scattered all around, yet doth it remain firm, for
its roots go down to the regions below, even as
far as its branches reach to heaven—so stood
Æneas firm, and, though he wept many tears,
changed not his purpose.

Then did Dido grow weary of her life. For
when she did sacrifice the pure water would
grow black and the wine be changed into blood.
Also from the shrine of her husband, which was
in the midst of her palace, was heard a voice
calling her, and the owl cried aloud from her
house-top. And in her dreams the cruel Æneas
seemed to drive her before him; or she seemed to
be going a long way with none to bear her company, and be seeking her own people in a land
that was desert. Therefore, hiding the thing that
was in her heart, she spake to her sister, saying, " I
have found a way, my sister, that shall bring him
back to me or set me free from him. Near the
shore of the Great Sea, where the Æthiopians
dwell, is a priestess, who guards the temple of the
daughters of Hesperus, being wont to feed the

dragons that kept the apples of gold. She is able by her charms to loose the heart from care or to bind it, and to stay rivers also, and to turn the courses of the stars, and to call up the spirits of the dead. Do thou, therefore—for this is what the priestess commands—build a pile in the open court, and put thereon the sword which he left hanging in our chamber, and the garments he wore, and the couch on which he lay, even all that was his, so that they may perish together."

And when these things were done—for Anna knew not of her purpose—and also an image of Æneas was laid upon the pile, the priestess, with her hair unbound, called upon all the gods that dwell below, sprinkling thereon water that was drawn, she said, from the lake of Avernus, and scattering evil herbs that had been cut at the full moon with a sickle of bronze. Dido also, with one foot bare and her garments loosened, threw meal upon the fire and called upon the Gods, if haply there be any, that look upon those that love and suffer wrong.

In the mean time Æneas lay asleep in the hind part of his ship, when there appeared to

him in a dream the god Mercury, even as he
had seen him when he brought the command-
ment of Jupiter. And Mercury spake, saying,
"Son of Venus, canst thou sleep? seest thou
not what perils surround thee, nor hearest how
the favourable west wind calls? The queen
purposes evil against thee. If thou lingerest
till the morning come thou wilt see the shore
covered with them that wish thee harm. Fly,
then, and tarry not; for a woman is ever of
many minds."

Then did Æneas in great fear start from his
sleep, and call his companions, saying, "Wake,
and sit on the benches, and loose the sails. 'Tis
a god thus bids us fly." And even as he spake
he cut the cable with his sword. And all hasted
to follow him, and sped over the sea.

And now it was morning, and Queen Dido,
from her watch - tower, saw the ships upon the
sea. Then she smote upon her breast and tore
her hair, and cried, "Shall this stranger mock
us thus? Hasten to follow him. Bring down
the ships from the docks, make ready sword and
fire. And this was the man who bare upon his
shoulders his aged father! Why did I not tear

him to pieces, and slay his companions with the sword, and serve up the young Ascanius at his meal ? And if I had perished, what then ? for I die to-day. O Sun, that regardest all the earth, and Juno, that carest for marriage bonds, and Hecate, Queen of the dead, and ye Furies that take vengeance on evildoers, hear me. If it be ordered that he reach this land, yet grant that he suffer many things from his enemies, and be driven from his city, and beg for help from strangers, and see his people cruelly slain with the sword ; and, when he shall have made peace on ill conditions, that he enjoy not long his kingdom, but die before his day, and lie unburied on the plain. And ye, men of Tyre, hate his children and his people for ever. Let there be no love or peace between you. And may some avenger arise from my grave who shall persecute the race of Dardanus with fire and sword. So shall there be war for ever between him and me."

Then she spake to old Barcé, who had been nurse to her husband Sichæus, " Bid my sister bathe herself in water, and bring with her beasts for sacrifice. And do thou also put a garland about thy head, for I am minded to finish this sacrifice which I have begun, and to burn the image of the man of Troy."

And when the old woman made haste to do her bidding, Queen Dido ran to the court where the pile was made for the burning, and mounted on the pile, and drew the sword of Æneas from the scabbard. Then did she throw herself upon the bed, and cry, " Now do I yield up my life. I have finished my course. I have built a mighty city. I have avenged my husband on him that slew him. Happy had I been, yea too happy! had the ships of Troy never come to this land." Then she kissed the bed and cried, " Shall I die unavenged ? Nevertheless let me die. The man of Troy shall see this fire from the sea whereon he journeys, and carry with him an augury of death."

And when her maidens looked, lo! she had fallen upon the sword, and the blood was upon her hands. And a great cry went up through the palace, exceeding loud and bitter, even as if the enemy had taken Carthage or ancient Tyre, and the fire were mounting over the dwellings of men and of Gods. And Anna her sister heard it, and rushing through the midst called her by name, "O my sister, was this thy purpose? Were the pile and the sword and the fire for this? Why wouldst thou not suffer that I should die with thee? For surely, my sister, thou hast slain thyself, and me, and thy people, and thy city. But give me water, ye maidens, that I may wash her wounds, and if there be any breath left in her, we may yet stay it.

. Then she climbed on to the pile, and caught her sister in her arms, and sought to staunch the blood with her garments. Three times did Dido strive to raise her eyes; three times did her spirit leave her. Three times she would have raised herself upon her elbow; three times she fell back upon the bed, looking with wandering eyes for the light, and groaning that she yet beheld it.

Then Juno, looking down from heaven, saw that her pain was long, and pitied her, and sent down Iris, her messenger, that she might loose the soul that struggled to be free. For, seeing that she died not by nature, nor yet by the hand of man, but before her time and of her own madness, Queen Proserpine had not shred the ringlet

from her head which she shreds from them that die. Wherefore Iris, flying down with dewy wings from heaven, with a thousand colours about her from the light of the sun, stood above her head and said, "I give thee to death, even as I am bidden, and loose thee from thy body." Then she shred the lock, and Queen Dido gave up the ghost.

CHAPTER X.

Now were Æneas and the men of Troy far from land. And looking back they saw a great light, nor knew what it might be; only they feared some evil hap, knowing the rage that was in Dido's heart, and what a woman in her madness may do. And indeed the people of the queen were burning her body on the pile which she had made.

But lo! the sky grew dark overhead, and there were signs as of a great storm. And Palinurus, the pilot, cried from the stern, where he stood with the rudder in his hand, "What mean these clouds? What doest thou, Father Neptune?" And he bade the men clear the decks and put out the oars to row, and shift the sails to the wind. Then he spake to Æneas, saying, "Italy we may not hope to reach with this weather. No, not though

Jupiter himself promise it to us. But, if I remember me aright, the havens of Sicily are at hand, wherefore let us turn our course thither."

And Æneas answered, " It is well : for I see that the winds are contrary to us. And, of a truth, there is no land whither I would more gladly go, seeing that my father Anchises is buried there."

Then they shifted their course, and let their ships run before the wind, and so came with much speed to the land of Sicily. Now Acestes, who was king of the land, was the son of a woman of Troy, and, seeing them from a hill-top, he came to meet them, having the skin of a lion on his shoulders and a javelin in his hand, and refreshed them with food and drink.

The next day at dawn Æneas called the men of Troy together, and spake, saying, " It is a full year since we buried my father in this land, and this, if I err not, is the very day : which I will that we keep holy with festival ; for such, indeed, would I do were I wandering in the wilderness of Africa or shut up in Mycenæ itself. Now, therefore, seeing that we are in

a land that is friendly to us, let us keep it with
solemnity. And let us vow also that we will
keep it year by year in the land of Italy, if so
be that, having prosperous winds, we shall come
thereunto. Likewise, King Acestes gives to us
oxen, for every ship two : wherefore make merry
and rejoice. And if the ninth day from this be
fair, I will that there be games of running in a
race, and of throwing the javelin, and of shooting with the bow, and of boxing, and the like.
And now make ready for the sacrifice."

Then he put upon his head a wreath of his
mother's myrtle. And old Acestes did the like,
and the boy Ascanius, and the others. Then he
came near to the tomb of his father, and poured
out two cups of wine and two of new milk, and
scattered flowers, and said, " Hail to thee, my
father, whom the Gods suffered not to enter
with me into the land of Italy."

And even as he spake there came forth a
great snake from the depth of the tomb. Seven
coils he had, and on his body were spots of blue
and gold, and as many colours as are the colours of the rainbow in the clouds. And when
Æneas stood astonied, lo ! the snake passed

between the altars and tasted of the sacrifice and of that which had been poured out. And Æneas, doubting what this might be, made fresh offerings, two sheep, and two swine, and two black oxen, calling on the spirit of Anchises. And the men of Troy also brought gifts, and slew oxen for sacrifice, and feasted on the flesh, roasting it with fire.

And now the ninth day was come, and the sky was fair. Great was the concourse of people, for the name of King Acestes was famous in the land. Also many came to see the men of Troy, and some to strive in the games. First were the prizes put in the midst, three-footed tables for sacrifices, and crowns, and palms, and weapons, and purple garments, and talents of gold and silver; and then the trumpet sounded and called the people together.

And first of all was the race of ships. Four were they that strove together, Mnestheus with the Sea - Horse, and Gyas with the Chimæra, and Sergestus with the Centaur, and Cloanthus with the Scylla. Now far out in the sea was a rock, which is covered by the waves when the sea is rough, but stands above them if it be calm,

and upon it the cormorants love to bask. Here
did Æneas set a great branch of holm-oak as a
goal, that the ships should round it and so return.
First they cast lots for places, and the captains
stood upon the sterns, in purple and gold, and
the rowers had garlands of honour about their
heads and were anointed with oil. Thus they
sat upon the benches, holding the oars for a
stroke, and their hearts beat high with hope.
And when the trumpet sounded each ship leapt
from its place, and the sea foamed with the
strokes of many oars. And all the people
shouted aloud, having favour for this or for that
of the captains. And first of all came Gyas
with the Chimæra, and next to him Cloanthus
with the Scylla, for his men were indeed the
stronger, but the ship more heavy. And after
the Scylla came the Sea-Horse and the Centaur
at equal speed, now this one being foremost and
now that. But when they were now come near
the rock, Gyas, being in the first place, cried to
his helmsman Menœtes, "Why goest thou
overmuch to the right? Keep thou close to the
rock. Let others choose the sea if they will."
But Menœtes, fearing the hidden rocks, turned

ever the prow to the sea. Then a second time
cried Gyas, " Make for the rock, Mencetes."
And as he spake, the Scylla now came near,
taking the inner course between the rock and
his ship, and passed him by. Then was he
greatly wroth and wept for rage; and laying
hold of Mencetes he cast him into the sea, and
himself put his hand to the helm and turned it
to the rock. But Mencetes, being an old man
and weighed down with his garments, hardly
climbed upon the rock, and sat thereon. Loud
laughed the men to see him fall, and swim, and
vomit the salt water from his mouth. But when
Mnestheus with the Sea-Horse, and Sergestus
with the Centaur, saw what had befallen, they
hoped to pass the Chimæra in the race. Eagerly
strove the two together, and Mnestheus, seeing
that the Centaur was yet before him in the race,
ran among his men as they rowed, crying, " O
my friends whom I chose to be my comrades,
quit ye like men, even as ye did in the seas of
Africa and the Ionian waves. The first place I
seek not, but last I would not return." And
the men strove with all their might, bending
forward to the stroke. And even then chance

gave them that which they desired. For the
Centaur, being steered too close, struck on a jut-
ting piece of the rock, and the oars were broken,
and the prow stuck fast. And while the men,
with poles and the like, were thrusting her forth,
Mnestheus with the Sea-Horse had gained the
open sea. And first he overtakes Gyas in the
Chimæra, and vanquishes it, seeing that it had
lost its helmsman. And now only Cloanthus
with the Scylla remains, and upon him also he
presses hard. Then did all the people cry aloud,
bidding Mnestheus make good speed that he
might take the first place. And the one were
loath to lose that which they had gained, and the
others having done much would do yet more, and
would give their lives so that they might prevail.
And now, perchance, had the two been equal for
the first prize, but Cloanthus stretched forth his
hands to the sea and prayed to the Gods that
have power therein. " Gods of the sea, wherein
I hold my course, help me now, so will I slay a
milk-white bull at your altars, and cast the
entrails into the waves, and pour clear wine
therewith." And all the band of the Nereïds
heard him, and the virgin Panopeä ; and Portum-

nus himself with mighty hand drave the vessel forward swifter than the south wind or an arrow from the bow, so that it first touched the shore. Then a herald cried aloud that Cloanthus with the Scylla had won the mastery in the race, and bound a garland of bay about his head. Then to the rowers Æneas gave three oxen, and jars of wine, and a talent of silver; and to the captains gifts for themselves; to the first a scarf broidered with gold with a double border of purple, and on it was wrought the royal boy Ganymede, as he hunted on Mount Ida. Eager was he, and as one that panted in the chase; but on the other side the eagle bare him away, and the old men that had charge of him stretched out their hands and the dogs barked fiercely to the sky. And to the second Æneas gave a hauberk of chain-mail with rings of gold, which he had himself taken from Demoleon by the river of Simoïs. Scarce could his two servants carry it, so heavy was it; yet Demoleon had worn it, and chased the men of Troy, running at full speed. And the third prize was two cauldrons of bronze and cups of silver embossed. But when all had departed

rejoicing with their gifts, lo! Sergestus came
creeping home with his ship, which he had scarce
won from the rocks, disabled, with one tier of
rowers, even as a serpent which a wheel has
maimed upon the road, which with his fore part
lifts himself up and threatens, but his hind part
trails upon the ground. So came Sergestus
back to the haven, and to him Æneas gave also
his reward, seeing that he had brought back ship
and crew, even a woman of Crete, Pholoé by
name, very skilful in the work of the loom.

After this Æneas chose him out a level space,
with woods about it, and having sat down in
the midst upon a throne, caused it to be pro-
claimed that all should come who would contend together in running. And many came,
both men of Troy and Sicilians. First of all
Euryalus, a comely youth, and Nisus with him
(now between these two was great love) ; next,
Diores, of the house of Priam, then Salius and
Patron, Greeks both of them ; and two young
hunters, Helymus and Panopes, who were of
Sicily and of the court of Acestes, and many
others also. Then said Æneas, " To each will
I give two javelins of Crete and an axe orna-

mented with silver, so that none may depart
without a gift. And the first three shall have
crowns of olive. Also to the first will I give
a horse with his furniture, and to the second a
quiver after the fashion of the Amazons, with
arrows of Thrace, and to fasten it a belt embossed with gold, and a jewel for a clasp
thereon. And let the third take this helmet of
Greece, and be content."

Then, when they had ranged them in a line,
and the sign was given, they ran. And for a
while all were near together. Then Nisus outran the rest ; and next to him was Salius, but
with a great space between, and the third
Euryalus ; and after him Helymus, and Diores
pressing close upon him, even leaning over his
shoulder and ready to outrun him had the
course been longer. And now were they at the
very end, when Nisus slipped in the blood of an
ox which chanced to have been slain in the
place, and kept not his feet, but fell, fouling
himself with blood and mire. Yet did he not
forget Euryalus whom he loved, but lifted himself from the ground and tripped Salius, so that
he also rolled upon the earth. So came Euryalus

first to the post, and Helymus next, and Diores the third. But Salius made loud complaint to all the assembly, great and small, that he had been vanquished by fraud; yet the people favoured Euryalus, for he was fair to look upon, and fairness ever commendeth virtue. Also Diores was urgent, who else had not won the third prize. Then said Father Æneas, "I change not the order; as each reached the goal so shall each take his prize. Yet may I pity him who suffered wrongfully." And he gave to Salius the great skin of an African lion, with shaggy hair and claws covered with gold. Then said Nisus, "Yet, if thou givest such prizes to the vanquished and hast such pity on them that fall, what hast thou for me? For surely I had won the first reward but for the ill fortune which Salius also accuseth." And he showed his face and body foul with mire. And the kindly prince laughed, and gave him a shield, the work of Didymaon.

CHAPTER XI.

THEN did Æneas offer rewards for boxers: for the conqueror an ox with gilded horns; for the vanquished a sword and helmet. Straightway rose up the huge Dares, who only had dared to stand in the lists against Prince Paris, and also at the funeral games of Hector had vanquished Butes, hurting him so sore that he died. (This Butes was of the race of Amycus, the great boxer whom Pollux slew, and no man had stood before him.) But when they saw the broad shoulders of the man and his might there was not found one to contend with him. Therefore Dares came near to Æneas, and, laying his left hand on the horns of the ox, spake, saying, "If there be no man to stand against me, why do I tarry? Bid them bring the prize." Thereupon Acestes rebuked Entellus, who sat near him upon the grass: "Sufferest thou such gifts to be taken

without contest? What of Eryx, thy master?
What of thy fame, which hath gone through all
the land of Sicily, and the spoils that hang in
thy house?"

Then said Entellus, "Think not, Acestes,
that I am fearful, or careless of honour. But I
am old: my strength is gone from me. Were I
young, as that boaster yonder, I had not waited
for gifts that I should go forth to the battle."

Then cast he into the midst two gauntlets
which Eryx, the great boxer, had been wont to
wear. And all men marvelled to see them, so
huge were they, and heavy with bull's hide and
lead and iron. And Dares stood astonied, nor
would stand against such arms. And when
Æneas regarded them and tried their weight,
Entellus spake, saying, "What had the man of
Troy said had he seen the gauntlets of Hercules
himself, and the dreadful battle that befell on this
very shore? These gauntlets Eryx, who was my
mother's son, was wont to wear: thou seest them
stained yet with blood and brains, and I also was
wont to wear them in the days of my youth. But
if Dares liketh them not, be it so; I put them
away, and he shall do the like with his."

Then he threw his garment from his shoulders, showing his mighty arms and sinews. And Æneas gave the two equal gauntlets, and they stood with heads thrown back, and began the battle. Dares indeed was swifter to move, and vigorous, and young; and Entellus was huge of stature, but slow and scant of breath. Many blows they aimed at each other: many times one smote the other on his breast or his cheek, but struck not home. And ever Entellus abode in the same place, swaying himself hither and thither with watchful eyes. But Dares was as one who besieges a city or a fort on the hills, and tries now this approach, now that, and searches out all the place, and assails it in many ways. But at the last Entellus lifted his right hand and dealt a mighty blow, which the other, foreseeing it as it fell, avoided; so that the old man wasted his strength in air, and fell with a great crash to the earth, even as falls a pine torn up by the roots on Mount Erymanthus or Mount Ida. Then the men of Troy and the men of Sicily rose up from their places to see the thing; Acestes also ran forward and lifted up the old man from the

earth and would have comforted him.   But he
went back in great wrath to the battle, anger
and shame stirring him up.   And Dares fled
before him over the plain, and he followed him,
smiting him now with the right hand, now with
the left, and his blows were as the hail that rattles
upon the roof.   But Æneas bade him stay his
anger, and spake kindly to Dares, bidding him
cease from the battle.   "Seest thou not that
this day the victory is another's, and that the
Gods are against thee ?   Fight not against the
Gods."   Then he commanded that the battle
should cease. And the companions of Dares led
him to the ships, scarcely dragging his legs, and
vomiting thick blood from his mouth, and teeth
in the blood.   Also they took the shield and
helmet which were his reward, but the palm-
branch and the ox they left to Entellus.   Then
said the conqueror, "See, son of the goddess,
and ye men of Troy, what strength dwelt in
this body while I was yet young, and from what
a death ye have saved this Dares." Then stood
he over against the ox and smote it with his
gauntlet between the horns.   And it fell dead
upon the earth.   And Entellus cried aloud, "O

ENTELLUS KILLING THE BULL

Eryx, I offer thee this life for the life of Dares,
being indeed the better for the worse. And I
lay aside these gauntlets and this art."

Next Æneas called for those who would
shoot with the bow, setting up a mast from the
ship of Sergestus, and fastening thereto a dove
by a cord, at which mast were all to shoot.
Then came the men together and cast lots,
drawing them from the helmet. And first
came Hippocoön, son of Hyrtacus; and next to
him Mnestheus ; and third Eurytion, brother of
Pandarus, who broke the treaty between the
men of Troy and the Greeks, shooting his
arrow at Menelaüs ; but the lot of Acestes
lingered in the helmet and leapt not forth.
Then first Hippocoön drew his bow and smote
the mast, so that it shook, and the bird fluttered
his wings in fear ; and next Mnestheus shot his
arrow, and the bird he touched not, but the
string which bound it he cut ; and Eurytion let
fly, calling the while on his brother Pandarus,
the mighty archer, to help him, and smote the
dove as she flew rejoicing through the air, so
that she fell to the earth and the arrow in her
body. And only Acestes was left, not having

whereat he should aim ; yet shot he into the
air, for he would show his skill and the might of
his bow.   Then lo ! a marvel befell, whereof in
after days men knew the fulfilment ; for the
arrow burned as it sped through the air, leaving
a line of fire, till it was altogether consumed,
even as a star that shoots across the sky by
night.   And men marvelled to see it, and
prayed to the Gods that it might be well. Then
great Æneas refused not the omen, but embraced Acestes and gave him many gifts, saying, " Take these gifts, my father, for Jupiter
willeth that thou shouldst have especial honour
in this thing.   I give thee, therefore, this bowl,
embossed with figures of men.   Old Anchises
had it, and to him Cisseus, who was the father
of Queen Hecuba, gave it."   Also he put a
crown of bay upon his head.   Nor did the good
Eurytion murmur, though he had slain the
bird ; the others also had their gifts and were
content.

Not even now was the assembly dismissed,
there remaining yet another sight to behold.
For Ascanius and the youths that were his
companions came riding on horses, and each

had a wreath about his head. Each also
had two javelins of cornel wood, and some had
quivers on their shoulders, and each a collar
of gold that lay on the top of his breast. Three
companies there were, and to each a leader and
twelve that followed. And one of the leaders
was Priamus, son of Polites, called by the name
of his grandfather, on a horse that was black,
with pasterns of white and forehead of white;
and another Atys, whom Ascanius loved; and
third, fairest of all to behold, Ascanius, on a horse
of Sidon, which Queen Dido had given him;
but to the rest Acestes had given horses of
Sicily.

And when these came forth there was much
shouting and clapping of hands, and the men
of Troy rejoiced to see the lads, so like were
they to the famous men their fathers. Then, a
signal being given, the companies were divided
into bands, and these made as if they fought a
battle. For sometimes they would fly, and
sometimes would pursue, and sometimes
would ride altogether this way or that.
Many were their ways and movements, even
as are the paths of the Labyrinth in Crete.

9

Swift also were they and nimble, even as
dolphins which sport among the waves in the
Carpathian Sea or African. This custom did Ascanius teach to his people when he built the city
of Alba, and the men of Alba taught it to their
children after them, and mighty Rome learnt it
also, and kept it in the time to come.

CHAPTER XII.

BUT while the men of Troy were busy with
the games, Juno prepared mischief against them
in her heart, and sent down Iris, her messenger,
to accomplish it. Now the women sat apart on
the shore, and lifted up their voices and bewailed
the old man Anchises. But when they looked
upon the sea they lamented for themselves that
they had so much travel to accomplish, for they
were weary of the sea, and would fain have a
city to dwell in. Which when Iris perceived,
laying aside the semblance of a goddess, she
took upon herself the form of Beroé, the wife
of Doryclus, and went among the women of
Troy and spake, saying, "O unhappy, that ye
were not dragged to death by the hands of the
Greeks! For now the seventh summer is come,
and yet we journey over many lands and seas,

and seek this Italy which ever flies before us.
Here we have friends and kindred. What forbids that we build here a city ? Shall I never
see the walls of another Troy, nor find Xanthus
and Simoïs, rivers of Troy, in a strange land ?
Why burn we not these accursed ships that
carry us hither and thither. I saw in a dream
the seeress Cassandra, and she seemed to put
a torch in my hand, and to say, ' Here seek
ye for Troy: here is your home.' And lo!
here are altars and fire."

Then she caught a brand from an altar, and
cast it far from her at the ships. Then cried
out Pyrgo, who had been nurse to the sons of
Priam, " O mothers of Troy, this is not Beroé
whom ye see. Mark ye her shining eyes, and
her voice, and her gait. But as for Beroé I left
her long since, sick and sore vexed that she was
absent this day from our solemnity."

And for a while the women stood in doubt regarding the ships, loving indeed the land whereon
they stood, yet knowing that the Fates called
them to another. But when the goddess rose on
her wings, and passed up by the path of the rainbow into the heavens, then a great fury fell upon

them, so that they caught brands from the altars
and set fire to the ships.   And straightway the
flames ran over the benches and the oars and
the stems of painted pine.   Then ran Eumelus
to the men of Troy where they sat at the games,
and told them how that the ships were burning;
also they themselves saw the black cloud of
smoke rolling before the wind.   And Ascanius, in
the midst of his horsemanship, heard the matter
and sped to the camp.   And being come he
cried aloud, "What madness is this ? Ye burn
not the camp of the Greeks, ye burn our own
hopes. Lo! I am your Ascanius." And he threw
his helmet on the ground, that they should know
him.   Also Æneas and the men of Troy made
haste to come up.   Then were the women
ashamed of that which they had done, and
would have hidden themselves, their fury being
past.   But not the more did the flame cease to
devour the ships ; and they who would have
quenched the fire availed nothing.   Then the
pious Æneas rent his garments and prayed to
the Gods, saying, " O Jupiter, if thou dost not
altogether hate us, save our ships from the fire,
and suffer us not to perish utterly ; but if thou

art angry, and so it seem good to thee, slay me
with thy thunderbolt."

And even as he spake there came up a great
storm from the south, with thunder and lightning
and a great rain, and the fire was quenched,
but of the ships four were burnt altogether.

Now Æneas was sore troubled at these things,
and doubted much whether he should still abide
in the land of Sicily nor heed the Fates, or should
yet follow after Italy. Then the old man,
Nautes, the priest of Pallas, in whom more than
in all men besides dwelt the wisdom of the
goddess, spake to him, saying, "Son of the
goddess, it must needs be that we go whither
the Gods call us. Yet mayest thou devise
something for this present necessity, taking
counsel with King Acestes, seeing that he also
is a son of Troy. For now, four ships being
burned, the people are over many for such as are
left to us ; some also faint at this thing that
we purpose ; also there are old men and women,
wearied of the sea, and the weak and the fearful.
Suffer, then, that he take these to himself to be
his people, and build a city for them, and call
it Acesta, after his own name.'"

And while Æneas thought on these things he slept.   And lo! in his dream there came to him his father, Anchises, and spake, saying, " I come, my son, at the bidding of Jupiter.   Take thou heed to the counsel which Nautes giveth thee, for it is good.   Let the chosen youth of thy people go with thee, for thou hast a mighty people and a fierce in Latium with whom to do battle.   But first must thou seek the dwellings of the dead and hold converse with me.   For indeed I dwell not in Tartarus, with the evil-doers, but in Elysium, with the companies of the blessed.   And thither shall the Sibyl guide thee, and thou shalt learn all that shall befall thee and thy people after this.   And now fare-well, for the morning cometh, and I must de-part."

And the spirit of Anchises vanished out of his sight, even as smoke into the air, nor heeded him when he would have stayed it; and Æneas arose and did sacrifice to the household gods and to Vesta.   Then he took counsel with his companions and with Acestes.   And Acestes heark-ened to his words.   And they separated such as would tarry in the place, both men and women; but the others, few in number indeed, but strong and of a good courage, made ready the ships to depart. And in the mean time Æneas marked the boundaries of the city with a ploughshare, and Acestes set it in order with laws and government. Also on the mountain of Eryx they built a temple to Venus, and they consecrated a grove and a priest at the tomb of Anchises.

Then for nine days they feasted; and after, for it was fine weather, and the south wind blew softly, they made ready to sail. There was then a great weeping and embracing on the shore; and now were all fain to go, willing not to be parted from kindred and friends. But Æneas comforted them, and, having sacrificed three calves to Eryx and a lamb to the Storms, so departed.

And Venus spake to Neptune, saying, "It troubleth me sore that Juno will not lay aside her wrath. For the city of Troy she overthrew, and, it being overthrown, she pursueth them that are left with hatred that cannot be appeased; and now I fear me much what she may do, for she stirred up Æolus that he loosed all the winds

against them ; and even now she put into the
hearts of the women this great madness that
they should burn the ships.   Wherefore I
pray thee that thou shouldest give them now
a safe voyage to Italy."   And the King of the
sea made answer, " Thou doest well to put thy
trust in my realms and me.   For both have I
stilled the madness of the sea and also on the
land have I taken thought for thy Æneas.
Mindest thou not the day when Achilles pursued
the men of Troy to their city, and filled the
rivers with dead bodies, so that Xanthus could
not make his way to the sea, and how Æneas
would have met him in battle, being weaker,
and I snatched him away in a cloud, yea though
I desired from my heart to overthrow the city
of Troy, even the works of my own hands ?
Fear not, therefore : he shall come safe to the
haven of Avernus.   One only of his company
must perish, even one life for many."

Then did he pass over the sea in his chariot,
and there was a great calm as he went, and the
clouds flew from the sky, and the great beasts
of the sea went with him ; also the gods and
goddesses of the sea, as Glaucus and Palæmon,

and the company of the Tritons and Thetis and the virgin Panopeä.

And the men of Troy loosed the sheets, and spread all the sails to the wind ; and the foremost of the fleet was the ship of Æneas, Palinurus being the helmsman. And in the night Sleep came down from the sky, and taking the shape of Phorbas, spake to Palinurus, saying, " All things are quiet ; rest awhile : it is the hour of rest. I will take thy office for thee." But Palinurus, scarce lifting his eyes, made answer : " Dost thou bid me trust calm seas and gentle winds ? Not so. Too often have I been deceived." Nor did he loose his hold upon the rudder, or take his eyes from the stars. Then did Sleep wave over him a bough that had been dipped in the water of Lethe ; and when he slept, as he must needs do, thrust him into the sea and a portion of the rudder with him ; and he fell, calling vainly for help.

And when the ships were close to the rocks of the Sirens, which in old time were white with bones of men, but now with spray and broken waves, Æneas perceived that the ship strayed from its course. For indeed, seeing that the helmsman had perished, the winds and the waves had their will of it. Then did he lay hold on the rudder himself, but it grieved him much that such mischance had befallen his friend.

CHAPTER XIII.

THE SIBYL.

So Æneas came to the land of Italy, nigh unto Cumæ, which was the dwelling-place of the Sibyl. And the men turned the forepart of the ships to the sea, and made them fast with anchors. Then they leapt forth upon the shore, and kindled a fire; and some cut wood in the forest, or fetched water from the stream. But Æneas went up to the great cave of the Sibyl, where, by the inspiration of Apollo, she foretelleth things to come.

Now the temple was a marvellous place to look upon. For Dædalus, when he fled from Minos, King of Crete, flying through the air upon wings, came northwards to the land of Cumæ, and tarried there. Also he dedicated his wings in the temple. On the doors thereof was set forth, graven in stone, the death of Androgeos, and the men of Attica choosing by

lot seven of their children who should be given
as a ransom yearly; and, rising from the sea
upon the other side, the land of Crete. Likewise the Labyrinth was there and its winding
ways; but Icarus they saw not, for when his·
father would have wrought the manner of his
death in gold his hands failed him : twice he
strove and twice they failed. And when
Æneas would have looked further, the priestess
said, " Linger not with these things, but slay
forthwith seven bullocks from the herd, and
seven sheep duly chosen out of the flock."
And when they came to the cave—now there
are a hundred doors, and a voice cometh forth
from each—the Sibyl cried, " It is time. Lo !
the god, the god !" And even as she spake
her look was changed and the colour of her
face; also her hair was loosened, and her breast
panted, and she waxed greater than is the
stature of a man. Then she cried, " Delayest
thou to pray, Æneas of Troy ? delayest thou ?
for the doors open not but to prayer." Nor
said she more. Then Æneas prayed, saying,
" O Phœbus, who didst always pity the sorrows
of Troy, and didst guide the arrow of Paris that

it slew the great Achilles, I have followed thy bidding, journeying over many lands, and now I lay hold on this shore of Italy, which ever seemed to fly before me. Grant thou that our ill fortune follow us no more. And all ye Gods and Goddesses who loved not Troy, be merciful to us. And thou, O Prophetess, give, if it may be, such answer as I would hear. So will I and my people honour thee for ever. And write it not, I pray thee, upon leaves, lest the winds carry them away, but speak with thy voice."

And for awhile the prophetess strove against the spirit; but at the last it mastered her, and the doors flew open, and she spake, saying, "The perils of the sea thou hast escaped, but there await thee yet worse perils upon the land. The men of Troy shall come to the kingdom of Lavinium. Fear not for that; yet will they fain not have come. I see battles, and the Tiber foaming with blood, and a new Xanthus and Simoïs, and another Achilles, himself also goddess-born. Juno also shall be ever against thee. And thou shalt be a suppliant to many cities. And the cause of all these woes shall be

again a woman. Only yield not thou, but go
ever more boldly when occasion shall serve.
Little thinkest thou that thy first succour shall
be from a city of the Greeks."

And when she had ended these words,
Æneas made answer: "O Lady, no toil or
peril shall take me unawares; for I have thought
over all things in my heart. But one thing I
ask of thee. Here is the door of the dwellings
of the dead. Fain would I pass thereby, that
I may visit my father. I carried him on my
shoulders out of the fires of Troy, and with me
he endured many things by land and sea, more
than befitted his old age. Likewise he bade me
ask this boon of thee. Do thou therefore pity
both father and son, for thou hast the power, if
only thou wilt. Did not Orpheus bring back
his wife from the dead, having his harp only?
Also Pollux goeth many times this same path,
redeeming his brother from death. And why
should I tell of Theseus and Hercules? And I
also am of the lineage of Jupiter."

Then the Sibyl spake, saying, "Son of Anchises;
it is easy to go down to hell. The door is open
day and night. But to return, and struggle to

the upper air, that is the labour. Few only
have done it, and these of the lineage of the
Gods and dear to Jupiter. Yet if thou wilt
attempt it, hearken unto me. There lieth hid
in the forest a bough of gold which is sacred to
the Queen of hell. Nor may any man go on this
journey till he have plucked it, for the Queen will
have it as a gift for herself. And when the
bough is plucked, there ever groweth another;
and if it be the pleasure of the Gods that thou
go, it will yield to thy hand. But know that
one of thy companions lieth dead upon the
shore. First must thou bury him, and after
offer due sacrifice, even black sheep. So shalt
thou approach the dwellings of the dead."

Then Æneas departed from the cave, and
Achates went with him, and much they won-
dered who it might be that was dead. And
when they came to the shore, lo! Misenus lay
there, than whom no man was more skilful to
call men to battle with the voice of the trumpet.
Hector's companion he had been in old time, and
then followed Æneas. And now, blowing his
trumpet on the shore, he had challenged the
gods of the sea to compare with him; wherefore

a Triton caught him and plunged him into the
sea, so that he died. Then did Æneas and his
companions prepare for the burial, cutting ilex
and oak and mountain-ash from the wood. But
when Æneas beheld the forest, how vast it was,
he said, " Now may the Gods grant that in this
great forest the bough of gold discover itself."
And as he spake, lo ! two doves flew before
his face, and settled on the grass, and he knew
them to be the birds of his mother, and cried,
saying, " Guide me now to the bough of gold,
and thou, my mother, help me as before." Then
the birds flew so that he could still see them
with his eyes, and he followed after them. But
when they came to the mouth of Avernus, they
sat both of them on the tree. And lo ! the
bough of gold glittered among the branches and
rustled in the wind. Right gladly did Æneas
break it off, and carry it to the dwelling of the
Sibyl.

In the mean time the men of Troy made a
great burial for Misenus on the shore, building
a pile of wood, and washing and anointing the
body. Also they laid the body on a bier, and
on it the garments which he had worn being

yet alive. Then others, with faces turned away,
held a torch to the wood, whereon also were
burned incense and offerings of oil. And when
the burning was ended they quenched the ashes
with wine. And Corynæus gathered the bones
into an urn of bronze, and purified the people,
sprinkling them with water with a bough of
an olive-tree. Then Æneas made a great
mound, and put thereon the trumpet of the
man and his bow; and the mountain is called
Misenus, after him, to this day.

But when the burial was ended he did as the
Sibyl had commanded. A great cavern there
is, from which cometh so evil a stench that no
bird may fly across. There they brought four
black oxen, and the priestess poured wine upon
their heads and cut hairs from between the
horns. And when they had burned these they
slew the oxen, holding dishes for the blood.
And Æneas offered a black lamb to the Furies
and a barren heifer to the Queen of hell,
smiting them with his sword. Then they burned
the entrails with fire, pouring oil upon them.
Then did the ground give a hollow sound
beneath them, and the dogs howled, for the

goddess was at hand. And the priestess cried, "Go ye who may not take part in this matter. And thou, Æneas, draw thy sword from its sheath and follow. Now hast thou need of all thy strength and courage." Then she plunged into the cave, and Æneas went with her.

CHAPTER XIV.

THE DWELLINGS OF THE DEAD.

So they went together through the land of
shadows, like unto men who walk through a
wood in a doubtful light, when the moon indeed
hath risen, but there are clouds over the sky.
And first they came to where, in front of the
gates of hell, dwell Sorrow and Remorse, and
pale Disease and Fear, and Hunger that tempteth
men to sin, and Want, and Death, and Toil, and
Slumber, that is Death's kinsman, and deadly
War; also they saw the chambers of the Furies,
and Discord, whose hair is of snakes that drip
with blood. And in this region there is an ancient
elm, in the boughs whereof dwell all manner of
dreams, and shapes of evil monsters, as many as
have been, such as were the Centaurs, half man
half horse, and Briareus with the hundred hands,
and others also. These Æneas, when he saw
them, sought to slay, rushing upon them with

the sword, but his guide warned him that they
were shadows only.

After this they came to the river of hell, whereon plies the Boatman Charon. A long white beard
hath he and unkempt; and his eyes are fixed in
a fiery stare, and a scarf is knotted upon his
shoulder, as is a pilot's wont. An old man he
seemeth to be, but hale and ruddy. Now there
was ever rushing to the bank a great crowd, wives
and mothers, and valiant men of war, boys, and
girls dead before they were given in marriage, and
young men laid on the funeral pile before their
parents' eyes. Thick they were as the leaves that
fall to the earth at the first frost of autumn, or
as the swallows, when they gather themselves together, making ready to fly across the sea to the
lands of the sun. And of these Charon would
take some into his boat; but others he would
forbid, and drive from the shore. This when
Æneas saw, he marvelled, and said, " O Lady,
what meaneth this concourse at the river?
What seek these souls? Why be some driven
from the bank and some ferried across?"

And the Sibyl made answer: " This river
that thou seest is the Styx, by which the Gods

in heaven swear, and fear to break their oath. Those whom thou seest to be driven from the bank are such as have lacked burial, but those who are ferried across have been buried duly; for none pass this stream till their bodies have been laid in the grave, otherwise they wander for a hundred years, and so at last may cross over."

Much did Æneas pity their ill fortune, and the more when he beheld Orontes and his Lycians, whom the sea had swallowed up alive before his eyes. Here likewise there met him his pilot Palinurus, to whom, when he knew him, for indeed he scarce could see him in the darkness, he said, "What god took thee from us and drowned thee in the sea? Surely, in this one matter, Apollo hath deceived me, saying that thou shouldst escape the sea and come to the land of Italy."

Then answered Palinurus, "Not so, great Æneas. For indeed to the land of Italy I came. Three nights the south wind carried me over the sea, and on the fourth day I saw the land of Italy from the top of a wave. And when I swam to the shore, and was now clinging to the rocks, my garments being heavy with

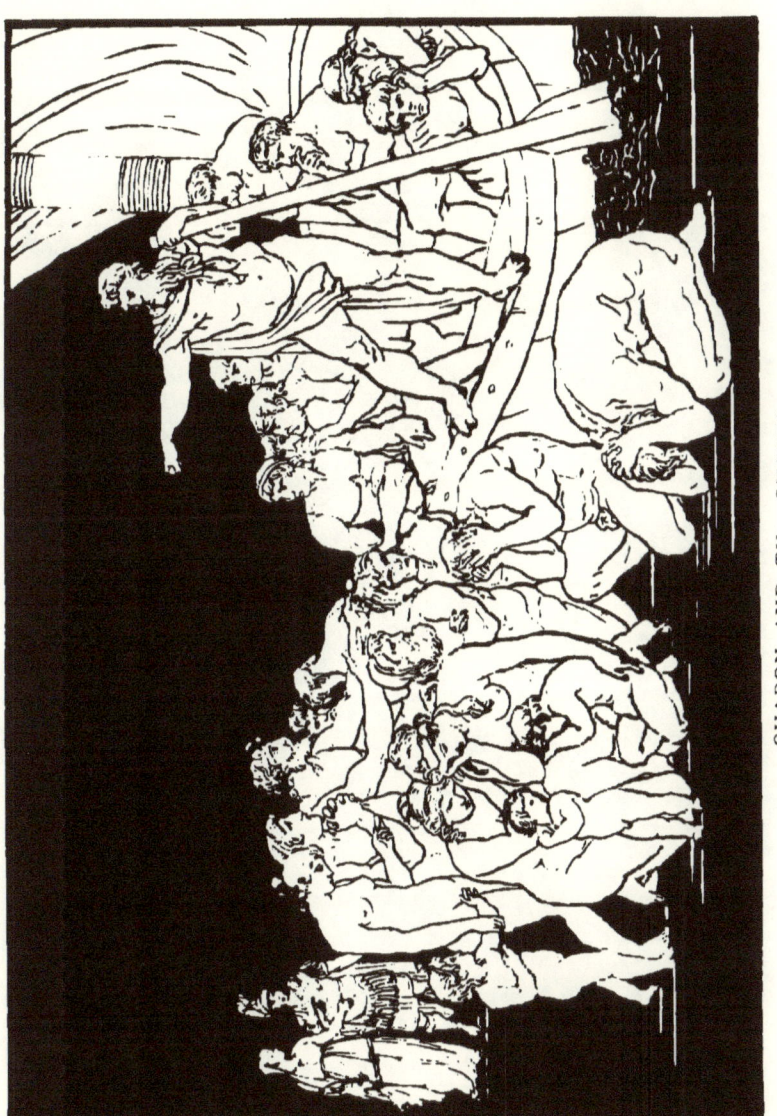

CHARON AND THE GHOSTS

water, the savage people came upon me, and took me for a prey, and slew me. And now the winds and waves bear me about as they will. Wherefore I pray thee, by thy father, and Iülus, the hope of thy house, that thou deliver me from these woes. Go, therefore, I pray thee, to the haven of Velia, and cast earth upon me for burial; or give me now thy hand, and take me with thee across this river."

Then said the priestess, " O Palinurus, what madness is this ? Wilt thou without due burial cross the river, and look upon the awful faces of the Furies ? Think not that the Fates can be changed by prayers. Yet hear this, and be comforted. They that slew thee, being sore troubled by many plagues, shall make due expiation to thee, and build a tomb, and make offerings thereon year by year ; and the place where they slew thee shall be called after thy name."

Then he took comfort and departed. But when they came near to the river, the Boatman beheld them, and cried, "Stay thou, whoever thou art, that comest armed to this river, and tell me what thou seekest. This is the land of

Shadows, of Sleep, and of Night. The living may
not be ferried in this boat. An evil day it was
when I carried Hercules, and Theseus, and
Pirithoüs, though they were children of the
Gods. For Hercules chained the Watch-dog
of hell, and dragged him trembling from his
master's seat. And Theseus and his friend
sought to carry away the Queen even from
the chamber of her husband."

Then the Sibyl made answer: " Be not
troubled. We came not hither with evil
thoughts. Let the Watch-dog of hell make the
pale ghosts afraid ; let your Queen abide in her
husband's palace ; we will not harm them.
Æneas of Troy cometh down to hell that he
may speak with his father. And if thou takest
no account of such piety, yet thou wilt know
this token."

And she showed him the bough of gold.
And when he saw it he laid aside his anger,
rejoicing to behold, now after many years, the
marvellous gift. Then he brought near his boat
to the bank, and drave out the souls that were
therein, and took on board Æneas and the
priestess. Much did it groan with the weight,

and the water poured apace through the seams thereof. Yet did they come safe across.

Then they saw Cerberus, the Watch-dog, in his cave. And to him the Sibyl gave a cake of honey and poppy-seed, causing sleep. And this he swallowed, opening wide his three ravenous mouths, and straightway stretched himself out asleep across the cave.

After this they heard a great wailing of infants, even the voices of such as are taken away before they have had lot or part in life. And near to these were such as have died by false accusation; yet lack they not justice, for Minos trieth their cause. And yet beyond, they that, being guiltless, have laid hands upon themselves. Fain would they now endure hardships, being yet alive, but may not, for the river keeps them in with its unlovely stream as in a prison. Not far from these are the Mourning Fields, where dwell the souls of those that have died of love, as Procris, whom Cephalus slew in error, and Laodamia, who died of grief for her husband. And among these was Dido, fresh from the wound wherewith she slew herself. And when Æneas saw her darkly through the shadows, even as one who sees, or thinketh that he sees, the new moon lately risen, he wept, and said, "O Dido, it was truth, then, that they told me, saying that thou hadst slain thyself with the sword. Tell me, Was I the cause of thy death? Loath was I, O Queen—I swear it by all that is most holy in heaven or hell—to leave thy land. But the Gods, at whose bidding I come hither this day, constrained me; nor did I think that thou wouldst take such sorrow from my departure. But stay; depart not; for never again may I speak to thee but this once only."

So he spake, and would fain have appeased her wrath. But she cast her eyes to the ground, and her heart was hard against him, even as a rock. And she departed into a grove that was hard by, wherein was her first husband, Sichæus, who loved her even as he was loved. After this they came to the land where the heroes dwell. And there they saw Tydeus, who died before Thebes; and Adrastus, and also many men of Troy, as the three sons of Antenor, and Idæus, who was the armour-bearer of King Priam, and bare the arms and drave the chariot yet. All

ÆNEAS AND THE SHADE OF DIDO.

these gathered about him, and would fain know wherefore he had come. But when the hosts of Agamemnon saw his shining arms through the darkness, they fled, as in old days they had fled to the ships; and some would have cried aloud, but could not, so thin are the voices of the dead.

Among these he saw Deïphobus, son of Priam. Cruelly mangled was he, for his hands had been cut off, and his ears and his nostrils likewise. Scarce did Æneas know him, and he himself in shame would have hidden his wounds; but the son of Anchises spake to him, saying, "Who hath dealt so foully with thee, great Deïphobus? Men told me that on the last night of Troy thou didst fall dead on a heap of Greeks whom thou hadst slain. Wherefore I built thee a tomb by the sea, and thrice called aloud thy name. But thee I found not, that I might lay thee therein."

Then Deïphobus made answer: "Thou hast left nothing undone, but hast paid me all due honour. But my ill fate and the accursed wickedness of the Spartan woman have destroyed me. How we spent that last night in idle rejoicings thou knowest. And she, while the women of Troy danced before the Gods, stood holding a torch on the citadel, as though she were their leader, yet in truth she called therewith the Greeks from Tenedos. But I lay overcome with weariness in my chamber. Then did she, a noble wife, forsooth! take all the arms out of the house, and my trusty sword also from under my head; and after brought thereunto Mene-laüs, so hoping to do away her sin against him; and Ulysses also, always ready with evil counsels. What need of more? May the Gods do so and more also to them. But tell me why hast thou come hither."

And it was now past noonday, and the two had spent in talk all the allotted time. Therefore the Sibyl spake: "Night cometh, Æneas, and we waste the day in tears. Lo! here are two roads. This on the right hand leadeth to the palace of Pluto and to the Elysian plains; and that on the left to Tartarus, the abode of the wicked." And Deïphobus answered: "Be not wroth, great priestess; I depart to my own place. Do thou, my friend, go on and prosper."

But as Æneas looked round he saw a great

building, and a three - fold wall about it, and
round the wall a river of fire. Great gates
there were, and a tower of brass, and the fury
Tisiphone sat as warder. Also he heard the
sound of those that smote upon an anvil, and
the clanking of chains. And he stood, and
said, " What mean these things that I see
and hear ? " Then the Sibyl made answer :
" The foot of the righteous may not pass that
threshold. But when the Queen of hell gave
me this office she herself led me through the
place and told me all. There sits Rhadaman-
thus the Cretan, and judges the dead. And
them that be condemned Tisiphone taketh, and
the gate which thou seest openeth to receive
them. And within is a great pit, and the depth
thereof is as the height of heaven. Herein lie
the Titans, the sons of Earth, whom Jupiter
smote with the thunder; and herein the sons of
Aloeus, who strove to thrust the Gods from
heaven; and Salmoneus, who would have mocked
the thunder of Jupiter, riding in his chariot
through the cities of Elis, and shaking a torch,
and giving himself out to be a god. But the
lightning smote him in his pride. Also I saw

Tityos, spread over nine acres of ground, and the vulture feeding on his heart. And over some hangs a great stone ready to fall; and some sit at the banquet, but when they would eat, the Fury at their side forbids, and rises and shakes her torch and thunders in their ears. These are they who while they were yet alive hated their brothers, or struck father or mother, or deceived one that trusted to them, or kept their riches for themselves, nor cared for those of their own household (a great multitude are they), or stirred up civil strife. And of these some roll a great stone and cease not, and some are bound to wheels, and some sit for ever crying, "Learn to do righteousness and to fear the Gods."

And when the priestess had finished these words they hastened on their way. And, after a while, she said, "Lo! here is the palace which the Cyclopés built for Pluto and the Queen of hell. Here must we offer the gift of the bough of gold." And this being accomplished, they came to the dwellings of the righteous. Here are green spaces, with woods about them; and the light of their heaven is fuller and brighter than

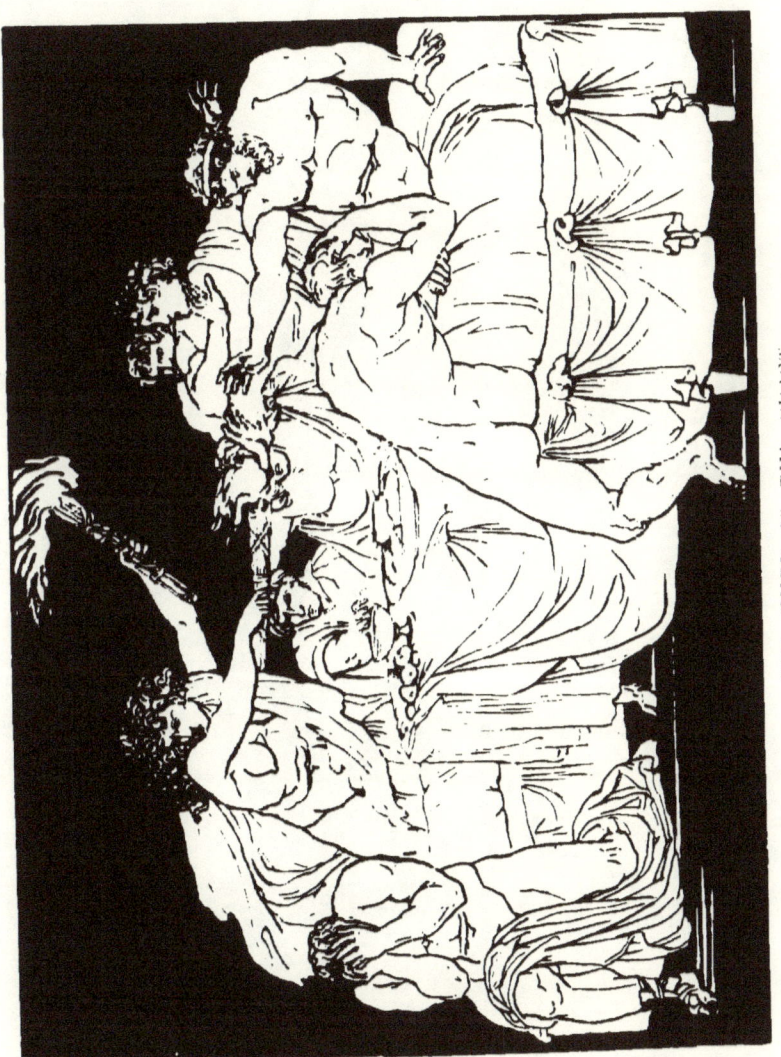

THE FURY AT THE FEAST

that which men behold. Another sun they have
and other stars. Some of them contend together in wrestling and running; and some
dance in measure, singing the while a pleasant
song; and Orpheus, clad in a long robe, makes
music, touching his harp, now with his fingers
and now with an ivory bow. Here did Æneas
marvel to see the mighty men of old, such
as were Ilus, and Dardanus, builder of Troy.
Their spears stood fixed in the earth, and their
horses fed about the plain; for they love spear
and chariot and horses, even as they loved them
upon earth. And others sat and feasted, sitting
on the grass in a sweet-smelling grove of bay,
whence flows the river which men upon the earth
call the Po. Here were they who had died for
their country, and holy priests, and poets who
had uttered nothing base, and such as had
.found out witty inventions, or had done great
good to men. All these had snow-white garlands on their heads. Then spake the Sibyl to
Musæus, who stood in the midst, surpassing
them all in stature: "Tell me, happy souls,
where shall we find Anchises." And Musæus
answered, "We have no certain dwelling-place:

but climb this hill, and ye can see the whole plain below, and doubtless him whom ye seek."

Then they beheld Anchises where he sat in a green valley, regarding the spirits of those who should be born in after-time of his race. And when he beheld Æneas coming, he stretched out his hands and cried, " Comest thou, my son ? Hast thou won thy way hither to me ? Even so I thought that it would be, and lo ! my hope hath not failed me."

And Æneas made answer, " Yea, I have come a long way to see thee, even as thy spirit bade me. And now let me embrace thee with my arms."

But when he would have embraced him it was as if he clasped the air.

Then Æneas looked and beheld a river, and a great company of souls thereby, thick as the bees on a calm summer day in a garden of lilies. And when he would know the meaning of the concourse, Anchises said, " These are souls which have yet to live again in a mortal body, and they are constrained to drink of the water of forgetfulness." And Æneas said, " Nay, my father, can any desire to take again upon them the body of death?" Then Anchises made reply: "Listen, my son, and I will tell thee all. There is one soul in heaven and earth and the stars and the shining orb of the moon and the great sun himself; from which soul also cometh the life of man and of beast, and of the birds of the air, and of the fishes of the sea. And this soul is of a divine nature, but the mortal body maketh it slow and dull. Hence come fear and desire, and grief and joy, so that, being as it were shut in a prison, the spirit beholdeth not any more the light that is without. And when the mortal life is ended yet are not men quit of all the evils of the body, seeing that these must needs be put away in many marvellous ways. For some are hung up to the winds, and with some their wickedness is washed out by water, or burnt out with fire. But a ghostly pain we all endure. Then we that are found worthy are sent unto Elysium and the plains of the blest. And when, after many days, the soul is wholly pure, it is called to the river of forgetfulness, that it may drink thereof, and so return to the world that is above."

Then he led Æneas and the Sibyl to a hill,

whence they could see the whole company, and regard their faces as they came; and he said, "Come, and I will show thee them that shall come after thee. That youth who leans upon a pointless spear is Silvius, thy youngest child, whom Lavinia shall bear to thee in thy old age. He shall reign in Alba, and shall be the father of kings. And many other kings are there who shall build cities great and famous. Lo! there is Romulus, whom Ilia shall bear to Mars. He shall build Rome, whose empire shall reach to the ends of the earth and its glory to the heaven. Seest thou him with the olive crown about his head and the white beard? That is he who shall first give laws to Rome. And next to him is Tullus, the warrior. And there are the Tarquins; and Brutus, who shall set the people free, aye, and shall slay his own sons when they would be false to their country. See also the Decii; and Torquatus, with the cruel axe; and Camillus winning back the standards of Rome. There standeth one who shall subdue Corinth; and there another who shall avenge the blood of Troy upon the race of Achilles. There, too, thou mayest see the Scipios, thunderbolts of war,

whom the land of Africa shall fear; and there
Regulus, busy in the furrows; and there the
Fabii, chiefly him, greatest of the name, who
shall save thy country by wise delay. Such, my
son, shall be thy children's children. Others
with softer touch shall carve the face of man
in marble or mould the bronze; some more
skilfully shall plead, or map the skies, or tell the
rising of the stars. 'Tis thine, man of Rome,
to subdue the world. This is thy work, to set
the rule of peace over the vanquished, to spare
the humble, and to subdue the proud."

Then he spake again: "Regard him who is
the first of all the company of conquerors. He
is Marcellus; he shall save the state in the
day of trouble, and put to flight Carthaginian
and Gaul."

Then said Æneas, for he chanced to see by
his side a youth clad in shining armour, and very
fair to look upon, but sad, and with downcast
eyes, "Tell me, father, who is this? How noble
is he! What a company is about him! but there
is a shadow of darkness round his head."

And Anchises made answer, "O my son,
seek not to know the greatest sorrow that shall

befall thy children after thee. This youth the
Fates shall only show for a brief space to man.
Rome would seem too mighty to the Gods should
he but live ! What mourning shall there be for
him ! What a funeral shalt thou see, O river
of Tiber, as thou flowest by the new - made
tomb! No youth of the race of Troy shall promise so much as he. Alas ! for his righteousness,
and truth, and valour unsurpassed ! O luckless
boy, if thou canst haply break thy evil doom
thou shalt be a Marcellus. Give handfuls of
lilies. I will scatter the bright flowers and pay
the idle honours to my grandson's shade."

Thus did Anchises show his son things to be,
and kindled his soul with desire of glory. Also
he showed him what wars he must wage, and
how he should endure, or, if it might be, avoid
the evils to come.

There are two gates of Sleep, of horn the
one, by which true dreams go forth ; of ivory the
other, by which the false. Then did Anchises
send forth his son and the Sibyl by the ivory
gate. And Æneas returned to the ships, and
making sail came to the cape which was afterwards called Caieta.

CHAPTER XV.

KING LATINUS

WHILE they tarried at Cumæ, Caieta, who was the nurse of Æneas, died and was buried ; and they called the cape after her name. And afterwards they set sail, and passed by the island wherein dwelt Circe, who is the daughter of the Sun. Pleasantly doth she sing, sitting at the loom, and burneth torches of sweet-smelling cedar to give her light by night. And round about her dwelling you may hear the growling of lions and wild boars and bears and wolves, which are men whom the goddess with her enchantments hath changed into the shapes of beasts. But Neptune would not that the men of Troy, being fearers of the Gods, should suffer such things. Therefore did he send them favourable winds, so that they passed quickly by that land.

Now when it was dawn, the wind being now

lulled, they came to a great wood upon the shore, and in the midst of the wood the river Tiber, yellow with much abundance of sand, flowing into the sea. And on the shore and in the wood were many birds. Thither the men of Troy brought their ships safe to land.

Of this country Latinus was king, who was the son of Faunus, who was the son of Picus, who was the son of Saturn. And King Latinus had not a son, but a daughter only, Lavinia by name, who was now of an age to be married. Many chiefs of Latium, and of all Italy, desired to have her to wife; of whom the first was Turnus, a very comely youth, and of a royal house. Now the queen, the mother of the virgin, loved him, and would fain have married her daughter to him, but the Gods hindered the marriage with ill omens and marvels. In the midst of the palace was a great bay-tree, which the king who builded the house had dedicated to Phœbus. On this there lighted a great swarm of bees, and hung like unto a cluster of grapes from a bough thereof. And the seers, beholding the thing, cried, " There cometh a stranger who shall be husband to Lavinia, and a strange people who shall bear rule in this place." Also when Lavinia lighted the fire upon the altar, standing by her father, a flame leapt therefrom upon her hair, and burned the ornament that was upon her head and the crown of jewels and gold, and spread with smoke and fire over the whole palace. Whereupon the prophets spake, saying, "The virgin indeed shall be famous and great, but there cometh a dreadful war upon her people." And King Latinus, fearing what these things might mean, inquired of the oracle of Faunus, his father, which is by the grove of Albunea. Now the custom is that the priest offereth sacrifice in the grove and lieth down to sleep on the skins of the sheep that he hath slain ; and it cometh to pass that he seeth visions in the night and heareth the voice of the Gods. So King Latinus, being himself a priest, made a great sacrifice, even of a hundred sheep, and lay down to sleep upon the skins thereof. And when he was laid down, straightway there came a voice from the grove, saying, "Seek not, my son, to marry thy daughter to a chief of this land. There shall come a son-in-law from beyond the sea, who shall exalt our name from the one end of heaven to the other." Nor did the king hide these things, but noised them abroad, and the fame thereof was great in these days when Æneas and his company came to the land of Italy.

Now it so chanced that Æneas and Iülus his son, and others of the princes, sat down to eat under a tree ; and they had platters of dough whereon to eat their meat. And when they had ended, and were not satisfied, they ate their platters also, not thinking what they did. Then said Iülus, making sport, "What! do we eat even our tables ?" And Æneas was right glad to hear this thing, and embraced the boy, and said, " Now know I that we are come to the land which the Gods have promised to me and to my people, that they would give us. For my father, Anchises, spake to me, saying, ' My son, when thou shalt come to a land that thou knowest not, and hunger shall constrain thee to eat thy tables, then know that thou hast found thee a home.' Now, therefore, seeing that these things have an accomplishment, let us pour out libations to Jupiter, and make our prayers also to my father, Anchises, and make merry. And in the morning we will search out the country, and see who they be that dwell herein."

Then he bound a garland of leaves about his head, and made his prayers to Mother Earth, and to the gods of the land, of whom indeed he knew not who they were, and to Father Jupiter, and to the other gods also. And when he had ended his prayer, Jupiter thundered thrice from the sky. Then was it noised abroad among the men of Troy that now indeed were they come to the land where they should build them a city; and they eat and drank and made merry.

The next day those who should search out the country went forth. And when it was told Æneas, saying that this river was the Tiber, and that the people who dwelt in the land were the Latins, valiant men of war, he chose out a hundred men who should go, with crowns of olive upon their heads, to the city of the king, having also gifts in their hands, and should pray that there might be peace between the men of Troy and his people. And the men made haste to depart; and in the meanwhile Æneas marked out for himself a camp, and bade that they should make a rampart and a ditch.

Now when they that were sent came nigh to the city, they saw the young men in the plain that was before it, riding upon horses and driving chariots. Others shot with the bow or cast javelins, and some contended in running or boxing. And one rode on horseback and told the king, saying that certain men in strange raiment were come. Then the king commanded that they should be brought into the palace, and sat upon the throne of his fathers, and gave audience to them.

Now the palace stood on the hill that was in the midst of the city, where King Picus had builded it, having woods about it very sacred. Here did the kings first receive the sceptre, that they should bear rule over the people. A senate-house also it was, and a banqueting-house, where the princes sat feasting. Very great was it and magnificent, having a hundred pillars; and in the halls were the statues of ancient kings, carven in cedar, even Italus, and Sabinus the vine-dresser, and Father Saturn, and Janus with the two faces. Also on the

wall hung trophies of war, chariots, and battle-
axes, and helmets, and javelins, and the beaks
of ships. And sitting on a throne was the
image of King Picus, clad in royal apparel,
bearing a shield on his left arm. But the king
himself his wife Circé had changed into a bird.

And King Latinus spake, saying, "Tell me,
men of Troy, for I know you who you are,
what seek ye? For what cause are ye come to
the land of Italy? Have ye gone astray in
your journey? or have the storms driven you
out of the way, as ofttimes befalleth men that
sail upon the sea? Ye are welcome. And
know that we be of the race of Saturn, who do
righteously, not by constraint, but of our own
will. From hence also, even from Corythus,
which is a city of the Etrurians, went forth
Dardanus, and abode in the land of Troy."

Then Ilioneus made answer, saying, "Great
King, we have not gone astray in our journey,
nor have storms driven us out of the way. Of
set purpose are we come to this land. For we
were driven away by ill-fortune from our country,
of which things we doubt not, O King, that thou
knowest the certainty. For who is there under

the whole heaven who knoweth not what a storm of destruction came forth from the land of Greece and overthrew the great city of Troy, Europe and Asia setting themselves in arms against each other ? And now are we come to ask for a parcel of land whereon we may dwell ; and for air and water, which indeed are common to all men. Nor shall we do dishonour to this realm, nor be unthankful for these benefits. And be sure, O king, that it will not repent thee that thou hast received us. For indeed many nations and lands would fain have joined us to themselves. But the Gods laid a command upon us that we should come to this country of Italy. For indeed, as thou sayest, Dardanus came forth from hence, and thither his children, Apollo bidding them, would return. And now, behold, Æneas sends thee these gifts of the things which remain to us of the riches which we had aforetime. This sceptre King Priam held when he did justice among his people ; here is a crown also, and garments which the women of Troy have worked with their hands."

Then for awhile King Latinus kept silence, fixing his eyes upon the ground. Deeply did he ponder in his heart upon the marriage of his daughter, and upon the oracles of Faunus his father, whether indeed this stranger that was now come to his land might haply be the son-in-law of whom the prophets had spoken. At the last he spake, saying, " May the Gods prosper this matter between you and me. We grant, men of Troy, that which ye ask. Also we regard these your gifts. Know ye that while we reign in this land ye shall not want for riches, even unto the measure of the riches of Troy. And for your king, Æneas, if he desire, as ye say, to join himself with us, let him come and look upon us, face to face. And also take ye back this message to your king. I have a daughter, whom the Gods suffer me not to marry to a husband of this land. For they say that there shall come a stranger who shall be my son-in-law, and that from his loins shall come forth those who shall raise our name even unto the stars."

Then the king commanded that they should bring forth horses from the stalls. Now there stood in the stalls three hundred horses, very fleet of foot. And of these they brought forth one hundred, one for each man of Troy; and they were decked with trappings of purple, and champed on bits of gold. And for Æneas himself he sent a chariot, and two horses breathing fire from their nostrils, which were of the breed of the horses of the Sun. So the men of Troy went back riding on horses, and took to Æneas the gifts and the message of peace.

CHAPTER XVI.

Now Juno beheld how the men of Troy were come to the land of Italy, and were now building them houses to dwell in ; and great wrath came into her heart, and she spake to herself, saying, " Of a truth this accursed race hath vanquished me. For the flames of Troy burned them not, neither hath the sea devoured them. And, lo ! they are come to the place where they would be, even to the river of Tiber. Yet could Mars destroy the whole nation of the Lapithæ, when he was wroth with them ; and Jupiter suffered Diana to prevail against the land of Calydon. Yet had not the Lapithæ or Calydon done so great wickedness as hath this nation of Troy. And I, who am the wife of Jupiter, am vanquished by Æneas ! Yet have I means yet remaining to me, for if the Gods of heaven will not help me, then will I betake me to the powers of hell.

From the kingdom of Latium I may not keep him, and the Gods decree that he shall have Lavinia to wife. Yet may I hinder the matter. Surely at a great price shall they buy this alliance; and thy dowry, O virgin, shall be the blood of Italy and of Troy."

Then Juno descended to the lower parts of the earth, and called to Alecto from the dwellings of her sisters the Furies—Alecto who loveth war and anger and treachery, and all evil deeds. Even Pluto hateth her, aye, and her sisters likewise, so dreadful is she to behold. And Juno spake to her, saying, "Now would I have thee help me, Daughter of Night, that I lose not my proper honour. I will not that Æneas should have the daughter of Latinus to wife, or dwell in the land of Italy. Seeing therefore that thou canst set brother against brother, and bring enmity into houses and kingdoms, that they should fall, break this peace that they have made, and bring to pass some occasion of war."

Then straightway Alecto betook herself to the dwelling of King Latinus. There found she Amata, the queen, in great trouble and wrath, for she loved not the men of Troy, and

would have Turnus for her son-in-law. And
the Fury took a snake from her hair, and thrust it
into the bosom of the queen. About her breast
it glided unfelt, and breathed poisonous breath
into her heart. And now it became a collar of
twisted gold about her neck, and now a crown
about her head, binding her hair. At the first
indeed, when the poison began to work, and her
whole heart was not as yet filled with the fever,
she spake gently and after the wont of a mother,
weeping much the while over her daughter.
"Art thou then ready, my husband, to give
thy daughter to this exile of Troy ? Hast thou
no pity for thyself, or thy daughter, or me ?
Well know I that with the first north wind he
will fly and carry her away over the sea. And
what of thy word, and of the faith that thou hast
pledged so many times to Turnus thy kinsman ?
If thou must seek a son-in-law from the land of
the stranger, I hold that they all be strangers
who obey not thy rule, and that the Gods mean
not other than this. And Turnus, if thou wilt
inquire more deeply into his descent, is of the
lineage of Inachus, and cometh in the beginning
from the land of Mycenæ."

12

But when she perceived that her husband heeded not these words, and when also the poison of the serpent had now altogether prevailed over her, she ran through the city like to one that is mad. Nay, she feigned that the frenzy of Bacchus was upon her, and fled into the woods, taking her daughter with her, to the end that she might hinder the marriage. Many other women also, when they heard this thing, went forth, leaving their homes. With bare necks and hair unbound they went, crying aloud the while ; and in their hands they held staves of pine, and were clad in the skins of wild beasts. And in the midst of them stood the queen, holding a great pine torch in her hand, and singing the marriage song of her daughter and Turnus ; and her eyes were red as blood.

Next after this the Fury, deeming that she had overthrown the counsels of Latinus, sped to the city of Turnus the Rutulian. Now the name of the city was called Ardea, and Danaë builded it in old time ; Ardea is it called to this day, but its glory hath departed. Now Turnus was asleep in his palace, and Alecto took upon her the shape of an old woman, even of Chalybé, who was the priestess of Juno; and she spake, saying, "Turnus, wilt thou suffer all thy toil to be in vain, and thy kingdom to be given to another? King Latinus taketh from thee thy betrothed wife, and chooses a stranger that he should inherit his kingdom. Juno commanded that I should tell thee this in thy sleep. Rise, therefore, and arm thy people. Consume these strangers and their ships with fire. And if King Latinus yet will not abide by his promise, let him know for himself what Turnus can do in the day of battle."

But Turnus laughed her to scorn. "That the ships of the stranger have come to the Tiber, I know full well. But tell me not these tales. Queen Juno forgetteth me not, therefore I am not afraid; but thou, mother, art old, and wanderest from the truth, and troublest thyself for nought, and art mocked with idle fear. Thy business it is to tend the temples of the Gods and their images, but as for war, leave that to men, seeing that it is their care."

Greatly wroth was Alecto to hear such words. And even while he spake the young man shuddered and stared with his eyes, for the

Fury hissed before him with a thousand snakes.
And when he would have spoken more, she
thrust him back, and caught two snakes from
her hair, and lashed him therewith, and cried
aloud, "Old am I! and wander from the truth!
and am mocked with idle fears! Nay, but I
come from the dwelling of the Furies, and war
and death are in my hand!"

And she cast a torch at the youth, and fixed
it smoking with baleful light in his heart. Then,
in great fear, he woke, and a cold sweat burst
forth upon him, and he cried aloud for his arms,
and was exceedingly mad for battle. Also he
bade the youth arm themselves, saying that he
would thrust the men of Troy out of Italy, aye,
and fight, if need were, with the Latins also.
And the people hearkened unto him, so fair was
he, and of noble birth, and great renown in war.

Then Alecto hied her to the place where
Iülus was hunting the beasts of the forest.
Now there was a stag, very stately, with exceeding great horns, which Tyrrheus and his
children had brought up from a fawn. And
Silvia, a fair virgin who was his daughter, was
wont to adorn it with garlands, and to comb

it, and to wash it with water. By day it would
wander in the woods, and at nightfall come
back to the house. This stag, then, the dogs
of Iülus having scented pursued, and indeed
Alecto brought it to pass that this mischief
shall befall ; and Iülus also, following hard upon
his dogs, shot an arrow at it, nor missed (for the
Fury would have it so), but pierced it through.
Then the wounded beast fled back to the house
which it knew, being covered with blood, and
filled it with a lamentable voice, as one that
crieth for help. And Silvia heard it, and cried
to the country folk for aid, who came forthwith, Alecto urging them (for the accursed
thing lay hid in the woods). And one had a
charred firebrand and another a knotted stick,
each such weapon as came to his hand. And
Tyrrheus, who chanced to be splitting a tall
oak with wedges, led the way, having a great
axe in his hand.

Then did Alecto climb upon the roof, and,
sounding with hellish voice through a clarion,
sent abroad the shepherds' signal. And all the
forest trembled at the sound, and Trivia's lake
and Nar, with his white sulphurous wave, and

the fountains of Velia ; and trembling mothers pressed their children to their breasts.

Then ran together all the country folk, and the youth of Troy hasted also to the help of Iülus. And now they fought not with clubs and charred stakes, but with swords and spears in battle array. Then Almo fell, the eldest of the sons of Tyrrheus, stricken in the throat, with many others round him, and among them the old man Galæsus, even as he offered himself to be a mediator between the two. Most righteous of men was he, and richest likewise, for he had five flocks of sheep and five herds of cattle, and tilled the earth with a hundred ploughs.

But Alecto, when she had accomplished these things, hasted to Juno, and spake, saying, " I have done thy bidding ; and now, if thou wilt, I will to the neighbouring cities, spreading among them rumours of wars." But Juno answered, " It is enough ; there hath been the shedding of blood. It were not well that the Father should see thee wandering in the upper air, wherefore depart, and if aught remain to be done, I will see to it."

CHAPTER XVII.

AFTER this the shepherds hasted back to the city, and bare with them the dead, even the youth Almo and the old man Galæsus, and cried for vengeance to the Gods and to the king. And fiercest of all was Turnus, complaining that men of Troy were called to reign over them, and that he himself was banished. And all the multitude was urgent with the king that he should make war against the strangers ; neither did any man regard the commands of the Gods. But the king stood firm, even as a great rock in the sea is not moved though the waves roar about it and the seaweed is dashed upon its sides. But when he saw that he could not prevail against these evil counsels, he called the Gods to witness, crying, " The storm strikes upon me, and I may not stand against it. O foolish Latins, ye shall pay for this madness with your blood, and thou, Turnus, shalt suffer the worst punishment of all; and when thou shalt turn to the Gods they shall not hear thee. But as for me, my rest is at hand ; I lose but the honours of my funeral."

It was a custom in Latium, which Alba kept in after time, and mighty Rome yet keepeth to this day, that when she beginneth to make war, be it on the men of Thrace or the men of the East, Arab, or Indian, or Parthian, they open the great gates of the temple (double they are, and made strong with bolts of brass and iron), on the threshold whereof sitteth Janus, the guardian. For the Consul himself, with robe and girdle, so soon as the fathers give their sentence for war, throws them wide, and the people follow the Consul, and the horns blow a great blast together. Even so they bade King Latinus, after the custom of his country, declare war against the men of Troy, and open the gates of slaughter ; but he would not, flying and hiding himself in darkness. Then did great Juno herself come down and burst asunder the iron-bound gates of war.

Then through the land of Italy men prepared

TURNUS OVER THE BODIES OF ALMO AND GALÆSUS

themselves for battle, making bright shield and spear and sharpening the axe upon the whetstone. And in five cities did they set up anvils to make arms thereon, head-pieces, and shields of wicker, and breast - plates of bronze, and greaves of silver. Nor did men regard any more the reaping-hook nor the plough, making new for battle the swords of their fathers.

Now the greatest of the chiefs were these :

First, Prince Mezentius, the Tuscan, who regarded not the Gods ; and with him Lausus his son, than whom was none fairer in the host but Turnus only. A thousand men followed him from Agylla. Worthy was he of a better father.

Next came, with horses that none might surpass, Aventinus, son of Hercules ; and on his shield was the emblem of his father, the Hydra, with its hundred snakes. Long swords had his men and Sabine spears ; and he himself had about his head and shoulders a great lion's skin, with terrible mane and great white teeth.

And from Tibur came two youths of Argos, twin brothers, Catillus and Coras, swift and strong as two Centaurs from the hills. And Cæculus, who builded Præneste, was there, son of Vulcan, and a great company of country folk with him, whereof many bare not shield nor spear, but slings with bullets of lead, and javelins in either hand, and helmets of wolf's skin upon their heads.

After him marched Messapus, tamer of horses, Neptune's son, whom no man might lay low with fire or sword; and the people followed, singing a war-song of their king, like to a great flock of swans, which flies with many cries across the Asian marsh. And next Clausus the Sabine, from whom is sprung the great Claudian house; and Halesus, companion of Agamemnon, and enemy of Troy from of old, with many nations behind him; clubs had they, fastened with thongs of leather, and wicker shields on their left arms, and their swords were shaped as reaping-hooks. After these came Œbalus, son of Telon, with the men of Campania, wearing helmets of cork, and having shields and swords of bronze; also Ufens, of Nersæ, with his robber bands; and Umbro, the Marsian priest, a mighty wizard and charmer of serpents, who also could heal their bite; but the wound of the Trojan spears he could not heal, nor did all his charms and mighty herbs avail him.

With them also came Virbius, son of Hippolytus, from Egeria. For men say that Hippolytus, when the curse of his father had fallen upon him, and he had perished by the madness of his horses, was made alive by the skill of Æsculapius, and that Jupiter, being wroth that a mortal should return from the dead, slew the healer, the son of Phœbus, with his thunderbolt; but that Hippolytus Diana hid in the grove of Aricia, that he might spend the rest of his days obscure and without offence. And therefore do they yet hinder horses from coming near to the temple of Diana. Nevertheless the youth Virbius drave horses in his chariot.

But chief among them all was Turnus, who moved in the midst, clad in armour, and overtopping them all by his head. And he had a helmet with three crests, and the Chimæra thereon for a sign; and on his shield was Io, with her horns lifted to heaven, and Argus the herdsman, and Inachus pouring a river from his urn. A great multitude of footmen followed him, Rutulians and Sicanians, and they that dwelt about the Tiber, and about Anxur, and about the green woods of Feronia.

Last of all came Camilla the Volscian, with a great company on horses, clad in armour of bronze. She loved neither distaff nor the basket of Minerva, but rather to fight and to outstrip the winds in running. And a mighty runner was she, for she would run over the harvest-field nor harm the corn, and when she sped across the waves of the sea she wetted not her foot therein. All the youth marvelled to behold her, and the women stood gazing upon her as she went. For a robe of royal purple was about her shoulders, and a snood of gold about her hair; and she carried a Syrian quiver and a pike of myrtle-wood, as the shepherds are wont.

CHAPTER XVIII.

So the chiefs were gathered together, and much
people with them, Mezentius, and Ufens, and
Messapus being their leaders. They sent an
embassy likewise to Diomed (for Diomed had
built him a city in Italy, even Arpi), to tell
him that Æneas and the men of Troy were
setting up a kingdom in these parts, and to bid
him take counsel for himself.

But Æneas was much troubled at these
things, and cast about in his mind where he
should look for help. And while he meditated
thereon he slept. And lo! in his dreams the
god of the river, even Father Tiber, appeared
to him. An old man was he, and clad in a blue
linen robe, and having a crown of reeds upon
his head. And he spake, saying, "Thou art
welcome to this land, to which thou hast
brought the Gods of Troy. Be not dismayed at

wars and rumours of wars, nor cease from thy
enterprise. And this shall be a sign unto thee.
Thou shalt find upon the shore a white sow
with thirty young, white also, about her teats.
And it shall come to pass that after thirty years
Iülus shall build him the White City. And
now I will tell thee how thou shalt have victory
in this war. Certain men of Arcadia, following
their king, Evander, have built a city in this
land, and called its name Pallantium. These
wage war continually with the Latins. To them
therefore thou must go, making thy way up the
stream of the river. Rise therefore, and offer
sacrifice to Juno, appeasing her wrath. And to
me thou shalt perform thy vows when thou
shalt have prevailed. For know that I am
Tiber the river, and that of all the rivers on
earth none is dearer to the Gods."

Then Æneas roused him from sleep, and
made his supplications to the Nymphs and the
river god, that they would be favourable to
him. And when he looked, lo! upon the shore
a white sow with thirty young, white also,
about her teats. Of these he made a sacrifice
to Juno. And after this he commanded that

ÆNEAS AND TIBER

they should make ready two ships, and so went on his way. And Tiber stayed his stream so that the men might not toil in rowing. Quickly they sped, and many trees were above their heads, and the image thereof in the water beneath. And at noonday they beheld a city with walls, and a citadel, and a few houses round about.

Now it chanced that Evander and his people were holding a sacrifice that day to Hercules before the city. But when they saw through the trees the ships approaching, they were astonished, and rose all from the feast. But Pallas, who was the son of the king, commanded that they should not interrupt the sacrifice, and, snatching a spear, he cried from the mound whereon the altar stood : " Strangers, why come ye? what seek ye? Do ye bring peace or war?"

Then Æneas cried from the stern of his ship, holding out the while an olive branch : " We be men of Troy, enemies of the Latins, and we seek King Evander. Say, therefore, to him that Æneas, prince of Troy, is come, seeking alliance with him."

Much did Pallas marvel to hear this name,

and said, "Approach thou, whoever thou art, and hold converse with my father;" and he caught him by the hand.

And when Æneas was set before King Evander he spake, saying, "I come to thee, O King, not unwilling or fearful, though indeed thou art a Greek and akin to the sons of Atreus. For between thee and me also there is kindred. For Dardanus, builder of Troy, was the son of Electra, who was the daughter of Atlas. And ye come from Mercurius, who was the son of Cyllene, who was also the daughter of Atlas. Wherefore, I sent not ambassadors to thee, but came myself, fearing nothing. Know thou that the Daunian race, which warreth against thee, pursueth us also; against whom if they prevail, without doubt they shall rule over Italy, from the one sea even to the other. I would, therefore, that we make alliance together."

And as he spake, Evander ceased not to regard him, and, when he had ended, spake, saying, "Welcome, great son of Troy. Gladly do I recognise the voice and face of Anchises. For I remember how Priam came of old time to the kingdom of his sister Hesioné, who was the wife of Telamon ; and many princes were with him, but the mightiest of them was Anchises. Much did I love the man, and took him with me to Pheneus. And he gave me when he departed a quiver and arrows of Lycia, and a cloak with threads of gold, and two bridles of gold, which my son Pallas hath to this day. The alliance that thou seekest I grant. To-morrow shalt thou depart with such help as I can give. But now, since ye be come at such good time, join us in our sacrifice and feast."

So they feasted together on the flesh of oxen, and drank wine, and were merry. And when they had made an end of eating and drinking, King Evander spake, saying, " This great feast, my friend, we hold not without good reason, which thou shalt now hear from me. Seest thou this great ruin of rocks ? Here in old time was a cave, running very deep into the cliff, wherein Cacus dwelt, a monster but half man, whose father was Vulcan. The ground thereof reeked with blood, and at the mouth were fixed the heads of dead men. Very great of stature was he, and breathed out fire from

13

his mouth. To this land came Hercules, driving before him the oxen of Geryon, whom he had slain. And when he had left these to feed in the valley by the river, Cacus, that he might fill up the measure of his wickedness, stole four bulls and four heifers, the very chiefest of the herd. And that he might conceal the thing, he dragged them by the tails backwards, so that the tracks led not to the cave. But it chanced that the herd made a great bellowing when Hercules would have driven them away in the morning. And one of the heifers which Cacus had hidden in the cave bellowed also, making answer. Then was Hercules very wroth, and caught up in his hand his great knotted club, and climbed to the top of the hill. Then was Cacus sore afraid, and fled to his cave swift as the wind, fear giving wings to his feet. And when he was come thither, he shut himself therein, letting fall a great stone which he had caused to hang over the mouth thereof by cunning devices that he had learned from his father. And when Hercules was come he sought to find entrance and could not; but at the last he saw one of the rocks that it was very high and leaned to

HERCULES AND CACUS.

the river. This he pushed from the other side, so that it fell with a great crash into the water. Then did the whole cave of Cacus lie open to view, horrible to behold, as though the earth were to open her mouth and show the regions of the dead. And first Hercules shot at the monster with arrows, and cast boughs and great stones at him; and Cacus vomited forth from his mouth fire and smoke, filling the whole cave. And Hercules endured not to be so baffled, but plunged into the cave, even where the smoke was thickest, and caught him, twining his arms and legs about him, and strangled him that he died. Of which deed, O my friends, we keep the remembrance year by year. Do ye, therefore, join in our feast, putting first wreaths of poplar about your heads, for the poplar is the tree of Hercules."

So they feasted; and the priests, even the Salii, being in two companies, young and old, sang the great deeds of Hercules: how, being yet an infant, he strangled the snakes that Juno sent to slay him, and overthrew mighty cities, and endured many grievous labours, slaying the Centaurs and the lion of Nemea; and how he went down to hell, and dragged the dog Cerberus therefrom, and many other things likewise.

And at even they went back to the city, and as they went Evander told Æneas many things concerning the country : how of old a savage race dwelt therein, living even as the beasts, whom Saturn, flying from his son Jupiter, first taught, giving them customs and laws ; and how other kings also had borne rule over them, and how he himself had come to the land at the bidding of Apollo. Also he showed him the city which he had founded, and the places thereof : very famous were they in after - time, when mighty Rome was builded, even on the selfsame ground. And when they came to his palace he said, " Hercules entered this dwelling, though indeed it be small and lowly. Think not, then, overmuch of riches, and so make thyself worthy to ascend to heaven, as he also ascended."

Then he led him within the palace, and bade him rest on a couch, whereon was spread the skin of an African bear.

CHAPTER XIX.

THE ARMS OF ÆNEAS.

VERY early the next morning the old man Evander rose up from his bed, and donned his tunic, and bound his Tuscan sandals on his feet, and girt his Tegean sword to his side, flinging a panther's hide over his left shoulder. Pallas, his son, also went with him. And two hounds, which lay by his chamber, followed him. For he would fain have speech with Æneas, whom, indeed, he found astir, and Achates with him. Then spake Evander: "Great chief of Troy, good will have we, but scanty means; for our folk are few and our bounds narrow. But I will tell thee of a great people and a wealthy, with whom thou mayest make alliance. Nigh to this place is the famous city Agylla, which the men of Lydia, settling in this land of Etruria, builded aforetime. Now of this Agylla Mezentius was king, who surpassed all men in wickedness.

For he would join a living man to a dead corpse,
and so leave him to perish miserably.   But
after awhile the citizens rebelled, saying that he
should not reign. over them, and slew his
guards and burnt his palace.   But on him they
laid not hands, for he fled to Prince Turnus.
Therefore there is war between Turnus and
Agylla.   Now in this war thou shalt be leader;
for as yet, when they would have gone forth to
battle, the soothsayers have hindered them, saying, 'Though your wrath against Mezentius
be just, yet must no man of Italy lead this
people; but look you for a stranger.'   And they
would fain have had me for their leader, but
I am old and feeble.   And my son Pallas also
is akin to them, seeing that he was born of a
Sabine mother.   But thou art in thy prime, and
altogether a stranger in race.   Wherefore take
this office upon thyself.   Pallas also shall go
with thee, and learn from thee to bear himself
as a warrior.   Also I will send with thee two
hundred chosen horsemen, and Pallas will give
thee as many."

And even before he had made an end of
speaking, Venus gave them a sign, even thunder

in a clear sky; and there was heard a voice as of a Tuscan trumpet, and when they looked to the heavens, lo! there was a flashing of arms.

And Æneas knew the sign and the intepretation thereof, even that he should prosper in that to which he set his hand. Therefore he bade Evander be of good cheer. Then again they did sacrifice, and afterwards Æneas returned to his companions, of whom he chose some, and them the bravest, who should go with him to Agylla, and the rest he bade return to Iülus, to the camp.

But when he was now ready to depart, Evander took him by the hand, saying, "O that Jupiter would give me back the years that are gone, when I slew, under Præneste, King Erulus, to whom at his birth his mother, Feronia, gave three lives. Thrice must he needs be slain, and thrice I slew him. Then had I not been parted from thee, my son, nor had the wicked Mezentius slain so many of my people. And now, may the Gods hear my prayer: If it be their pleasure that Pallas should come back, may I live to see it; but if not, may I die even now while I hold thee in my arms, my son, my one and only joy."

And his spirit left the old man, and they carried him into the palace. Then the horsemen rode out from the gates, with Pallas in the midst, adorned with mantle and blazoned arms, fair as the Morning Star, which Venus loves beyond all others in the sky. The women stood watching them from the walls, while they shouted aloud and galloped across the plain. And after a while they came to a grove, near to which the Etruscans and Tarchon, their leader, had pitched their camp.

Now in the mean time Venus had bestirred herself for her son, for while he slept in the palace of Evander she spake to her husband, even Vulcan, saying, "While the Greeks were fighting against Troy, I sought not thy help, for I would not that thou shouldst labour in vain; but now that Æneas is come to Italy by the command of the Gods, I ask thee that thou shouldst make arms and armour for my son. This Aurora asked for Memnon; this Thetis for Achilles, and thou grantedst it to them. And now thou seest how the nations

join themselves to destroy him. Wherefore I
pray thee to help me." And he hearkened to
her voice. Therefore when the morning was
come, very early, even as a woman who maketh
her living by the distaff riseth and kindleth her
fire, and giveth tasks to her maidens, that she
may provide for her husband and her children,
even so Vulcan rose betimes to his work. Now
there is an island, Liparé, nigh unto the shore
of Sicily, and there the god had set up his
furnace and anvil, and the Cyclopés were at
work, forging thunderbolts for Jupiter, whereof
one remained half wrought. Three parts of
hail had they used, and three of rain-cloud, and
three of red fire and the south wind ; and now
they were adding to it lightning, and noise, and
fear, and wrath, with avenging flames. And
elsewhere they wrought a chariot for Mars, and
a shirt of mail for Minerva, even the Ægis, with
golden scales as of a serpent, and in the midst
the Gorgon's head, lopped at the nape, with
rolling eyes. But the god cried, " Cease ye
your toils. Ye must make arms for a hero."
Then they all bent them to their toil. Then
bronze, and gold, and iron flowed in streams ;

and some plied the bellows, and others dipped the hissing mass in water, and a third turned the ore in griping pincers.

A helmet they made with nodding crest, that blazed like fire, and a sword, and a cuirass of ruddy bronze, and greaves of gold molten many times, and a spear, and a shield whereon was wrought a marvellous story of things to come. For the god had set forth all the story of Rome. There lay the she-wolf in the cave of Mars, suckling the twin babes that feared her not—and she, bending back her neck, licked them with her tongue; and there the men of Rome carried off the Sabine virgins to be their wives ; and hard by the battle raged, and there again the kings made peace together, with offerings and sacrifice. Also there were wrought the chariots that tore asunder Mettus of Alba for his treachery, and Porsenna bidding the Romans take back their king, besieging the city, but the men of Rome stood in arms against him. Angry and threatening stood the king to see how Cocles broke down the bridge, and Clœlia burst her bonds to swim across the river. There Manlius stood to guard the Capitol, and a goose of silver flapped his wings in arcades of gold,

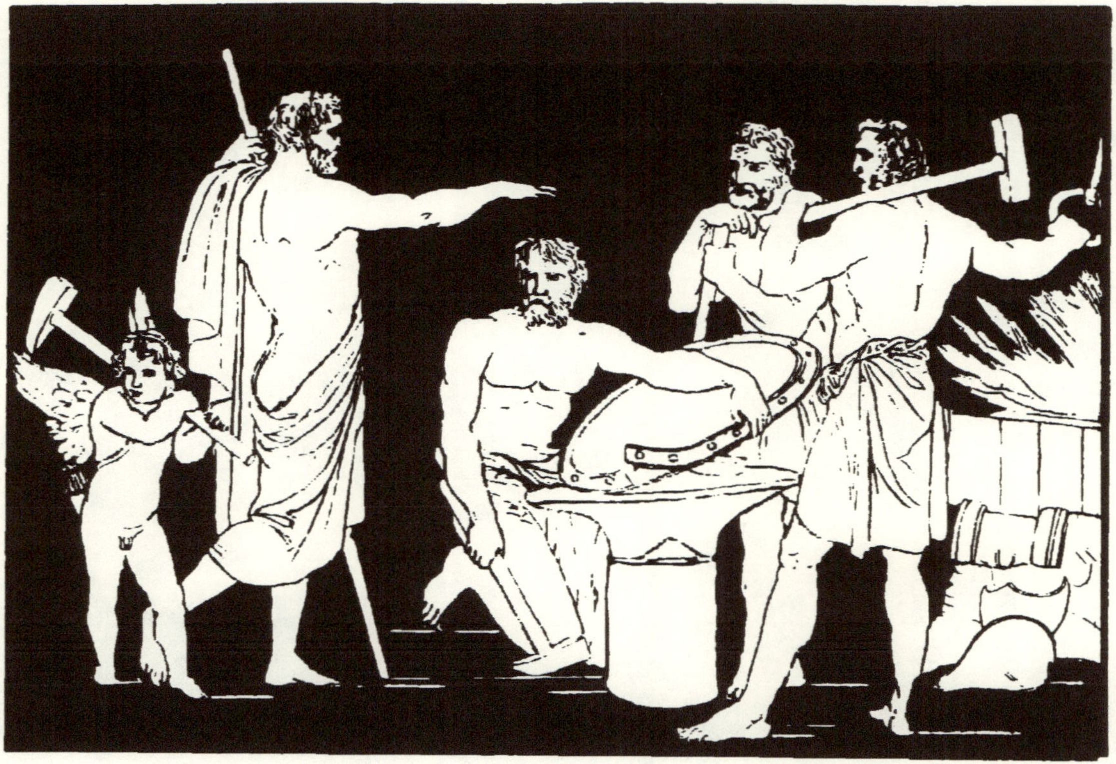

VULCAN AND TH[illegible] C[illegible]O

and showed the Gauls at hand. And they,
under cover of the darkness, were climbing
through the thickets even to the ridge of the
hill. Their hair was wrought in gold, in gold
their raiment ; and their cloaks were of divers
colours crossed ; milk-white their necks and
clasped with gold ; two spears had each and an
oblong shield. Likewise he wrought the dwellings of the dead, of the just and of the unjust.
Here Catiline hung from the rock while the
Furies pursued him ; there Cato gave the people
laws. And all about was the sea wrought in
gold ; but the waves were blue, and white the
foam, and therein sported dolphins of silver.
But in the midst was wrought a great battle of
ships at the cape of Actium. On the one side
Augustus led the men of Italy to battle, standing very high on the stern of the ship. From
either temple of his head blazed forth a fire.
And Agrippa also led on his array with a naval
crown about his head. And on the other side
stood Antony, having with him barbarous
soldiers arrayed in divers fashions, and leading
to battle Egypt and Persia and the armies of
the East ; and lo ! behind him—a shameful

sight—his Egyptian wife. But in another part
the battle raged, and all the sea was in a foam
with oars and triple beaks. It seemed as though
islands were torn from their places, or mountain
clashed against mountain, so great was the shock
of the ships. And all about flew javelins with
burning tow, and the sea was red with blood.
In the midst stood Queen Cleopatra, with a
timbrel in her hand, and called her armies to
the battle : behind her you might see the snakes
by whose bite she should die. And on one side
the dog Anubis, with other monstrous shapes
of gods, and over against them Neptune, and
Venus, and Minerva. And in the midst Mars
was seen to rage, embossed in steel; and the
Furies hovered above, and Discord stalked
with garment rent, while high above Apollo
stretched his bow, and Egyptian and Indian
and Arab fled before him. And in a third
place great Cæsar rode through Rome in
triumph, and the city was full of joy, and the
matrons were gathered in the temples; and
through the street there passed a long array
of nations that he had conquered, from the east,
and from the west, and from the north, and

from the south.   Such was the shield which
Vulcan wrought.

And Venus, when she saw her son that none
was with him, — for he had wandered apart
from his companions,—brought the arms and
laid them down before him, saying, "See the
arms that I promised I would give thee. These
my husband, the Fire-god, hath wrought for
thee.   With these thou needst shun no enemy ;
no, not Turnus himself."   Right glad was he to
see them, and fitted them upon him, and swung
the shield upon his shoulder, nor knew what
mighty fates of his children he bare thereon.

CHAPTER XX.

BUT Juno, ever seeking occasion against the men of Troy, sent Iris, the messenger of the Gods, to Turnus, as he sat in the grove of Pilumnus his father. Iris said, " That which none of the Gods had dared to promise thee, lo! time itself hath brought. Æneas hath left his companions and his ship, seeking the city of Evander, yea, and the Tuscans also. Do thou, therefore, take the occasion and surprise the camp while he is yet absent.

And she spread her wings and mounted to heaven by the arch of the rainbow, and Turnus cried, " I know thee, goddess, and follow thy sign." And having first washed his hands, he prayed and vowed his vows to the Gods.

So the army went forth to the battle. Messapus led the first line, and the sons of Tyrrheus the rear ; and in the midst was Turnus. And the

IRIS APPEARING TO THE KI

men of Troy saw a great cloud of dust upon
the plain, and Caïcus cried from the walls, "What
meaneth this cloud that I see? To arms, my
friends. Climb the walls. The enemy is at hand."
Then did the men of Troy shut the gates and
man the walls. For so had Æneas commanded
them, saying, "Fight not, whatever befall, in
battle, nor trust yourselves to the plain, but
defend your walls." Therefore they shut their
gates, and waited till the enemy should come
near. And Turnus, on a horse of Thrace, rode
first, and twenty youths with him ; and he cried,
"Is there a man who will first venture the
attack ?" and he threw his javelin, making a
beginning of battle, and his companions shouted
aloud. Much they marvelled that the men of
Troy kept them within the walls and came not
forth to the battle. And Turnus ever regarded
the walls, how he might enter therein. Even
as a wolf prowleth round the fold at midnight,
while the lambs within bleat, being safe by their
mothers, but he rageth without to hear them,
being mad with wrath and hunger, and his
tongue is athirst for blood, even so did Turnus
rage round the camp, and cast about how he

might draw forth the men of Troy into the plain. And at the last he bethought him of the ships, which lay at the camp's side, and called for torches of pine, and the people followed him with a shout, and the smoke rose up to the heavens.

Then did a marvellous thing befall. Now in the days when Æneas was building his ships upon Mount Ida, Cybele, mother of the Gods, spake to Jupiter, saying "Grant, my son, that these ships, which Æneas buildeth of my pine-trees,—for these have I given to him freely,—may be safe from winds and waves." But Jupiter answered, "What is this that thou askest, my mother? Wouldst thou have immortality for mortal ships? Not so. But this I grant: that whichsoever of these shall come safe to the land of Italy shall become Nymphs of the sea." And now the day was come. Wherefore there was heard an awful voice, saying, "Fear not, men of Troy; nor care to defend your ships;" and to the ships, "Go! henceforth ye are Nymphs of the sea." And lo! straightway the cables brake, and where the ships had been were the shapes of women, for each ship a woman.

Much did the Latins wonder to behold the thing, and Tiber stayed his stream to see it. But Turnus trembled not, crying, " This marvel meaneth evil for the men of Troy. Their ships abide not our attack. Nor have they any longer that wherewith they may flee from us. And as for fate, I heed it not. It was the fate of the men of Troy that they should touch the land of Italy. It is my fate that I should destroy the accursed race. They rob me of my wife. That wrong toucheth others besides Menelaüs. Surely, it had been enough to perish once. But why, then, will they sin again ? It had been well had they loathed thereafter all womankind. Or do they think that this rampart shall protect them ? Did they not see the walls which Neptune builded settle down in the fire ? And now, who cometh with me to storm their camp ? I need not arms from Vulcan's forge, or a thousand ships. Deeds of darkness and of stealth they need not fear. We will not hide us in a Horse of wood. In daylight will we burn their walls. For surely the youth of Italy is not as the youth of Greece, whom Hector kept at bay for ten years." Then he

14

commanded that they should lay siege to the camp; and Messapus he set to watch the gate, and fourteen Rutulian chiefs, with each a hundred youths, kept guard on the walls. So all the night they watched, and feasted, and drank, and made merry.

But the men of Troy laboured meanwhile, making strong the gates and the towers of the walls. And Mnestheus and Sergestus were instant with command and exhortation, for Æneas had appointed them to this thing should any need arise, he being absent.

Now the keeper of the gate was Nisus, a valiant man of war, and with him Euryalus, the goodliest youth among the men of Troy; and great love was between them. And as they watched, Nisus said, "Whether it be a bidding of the Gods, or prompting of my own heart, I know not, but I have a great desire to do somewhat this night. Seest thou how the enemy lie asleep and drunken? Can I not win some honour hence, and carry the tidings of these things to Æneas? For yonder by the hill lieth the way to the city of Evander."

Then Euryalus made answer: "Nay, but

thou goest not alone, Nisus, nor leavest me. My father Opheltes trained me not to such baseness, nor have I so borne myself in thy company. And truly I should count life well lost for such honour."

Then said Nisus : " I thought not so ill of thee. So may Jupiter bring me back in safety and honour. Yet should some mischance befall I would that thou yet shouldst live, to buy my body back, or, if that may not be, to pay due honour to my spirit. Think, too, of thy mother, who, alone of all the mothers of Troy, hath, for love of thee, come to this land of Italy."

But Euryalus said : " Thou makest idle excuses, for I am steadfastly purposed to go. Let us hasten, therefore." So they woke those who should take their places at the gate, and sought speech of the chiefs. These indeed were holding counsel, and stood leaning on their spears in the midst of the camp. And Nisus said that he had somewhat to say, and that the matter pressed. Then Iülus bade him speak ; and he made answer : " The enemy lie sleeping and drunken about the walls, and the fires are extinguished. If fortune favour us we will win a way to Æneas, to the city of Evander, and slay many, and take much spoil likewise. The way indeed we know, having learnt it while we hunted in these parts." Then the old man Aletes said: "Surely, Troy hath not altogether perished, having yet such hearts as yours." And he threw his arms about them, weeping. And Iülus said, "Bring back my father, and all shall be well. And I will give you two cups of silver embossed with figures of men, which my father took from the city of Arisba. And if we subdue this land of Italy, thou, Nisus, shalt have the horses and the arms of Turnus, and twelve women-captives likewise, and twelve men with their arms, and the domain of King Latinus. And thou, Euryalus, who art nearer of age to me, shalt be next to myself in all things."

Then Euryalus made answer: "One thing I ask thee more. I have a mother, of the lineage of Priam. To her I say not fare-well, not being able to endure her tears. Do thou care for her, if she be bereaved of me." And Iülus said: "She shall be as my mother to me."

Then he gave him his own sword, with its scabbard of ivory, and Mnestheus gave to Nisus a lion's skin, and Aletes a helmet. And all went with them to the gates, with many prayers and vows ; also Iülus, being wise beyond his years, sent many messages to his father.

Then they crossed the moat, and came upon the enemy as they slept, Nisus being before, and Euryalus keeping watch lest any should assail them from behind. And first Nis.ıs slew Rhamnes as he slept: an augur he was, whom Turnus most trusted, yet he knew not his own doom. Next he slew the three servants and the armour-bearer and the charioteer of Remus, and, after, Remus himself, cutting off his head. Others also he slew, and among them Serranus, a fair youth, who had been foremost in his sport that night. It had been well for him had he prolonged it even unto dawn. Many also did Euryalus slay, all of them in their sleep, save Rhœtus only, who, being awake, would fain have hidden himself behind a great jar, but could not. But when he would have assailed Messapus and his comrades, Nisus, seeing that he was mastered by the love of slaughter, cried aloud, "Cease: the day approacheth. It is enough that we have made us a way through the enemy." Much spoil did they leave behind them; but Euryalus took a sword-belt with knobs of gold from Rhamnes — Cædicus gave it to Remulus of Tibur, and he to his grandson, from whom Rhamnes had won it in war—and put on his head the helmet of Messapus. So they departed from the camp.

But it so chanced that three hundred horsemen, with Volscens their leader, were riding to the camp from the city. And as they came nigh, one of them espied, in the light of the moon, the helmet which Euryalus, being but a youth and unwary, had put on him. And Volscens cried, "Who are ye? Whither do ye go?"

But they answered nothing, making haste to fly. Then Volscens commanded that they should keep the wood on every side. Very thick it was with dark ilex-trees and brambles. And Euryalus, indeed, being laden with his spoil and fearful, wandered from the way, but Nisus got himself clear. But when he came to the stalls where they kept the cattle of King

NISUS AND EURYALUS

Latinus, he knew himself to be alone, and looked round for his companion, but saw him not. Then returning he searched through the wood till he heard the sound of horsemen approaching; and lo! Euryalus was in the midst, seeking to get free, but could not. Forthwith, having first prayed to Diana that she would help him, if perchance he might scatter this company, he cast his spear. It pierced the back of Sulmo, and passed even through his heart. And while they all looked, lo! another spear, and it pierced the head of Tagus from temple to temple. Very wroth was Volscens to see such slaughter, and know not how it befell; and he cried, " Thou at least shalt suffer for these deeds," and flew upon Euryalus. This could not Nisus endure to see, but rushed from his hiding-place, and cried, " Lo! I am the man who wrought this slaughter. Turn your swords against me. He did not, nay, he could not do such deeds. He did but follow his friend." But not the less did the sword of Volscens pierce the side of Euryalus; and the blood gushed out over his fair body, and his head drooped, even as a flower, which the ploughshare cuts in the field, or a poppy whose stalk is broken. Then rushed Nisus into the midst, thinking only how he might slay Volscens; nor could the enemy stay him, but that he thrust his sword into his mouth and slew him. And afterwards, being pierced with many wounds, he fell dead upon the body of his friend.

But when the horsemen were come to the camp, they found the slaughter that had been done. And when the day dawned they set the battle in array against the men of Troy, and the heads of Nisus and Euryalus they fixed upon poles, and showed them.

But when the report of these things came to the ears of the mother of Euryalus, she threw down her distaff, and hasted through the camp; and coming to the wall, she cried, " Is it thus I see thee, my son? Why was it not granted to me to bid thee farewell? And now I may not close thine eyes or wrap thee in the garments which I have made, solacing my cares with the labours of the loom. Slay me with your spears, ye Latins; or thou, great Jupiter, smite me with thy thunder, since I may not rid me otherwise of this hateful life."

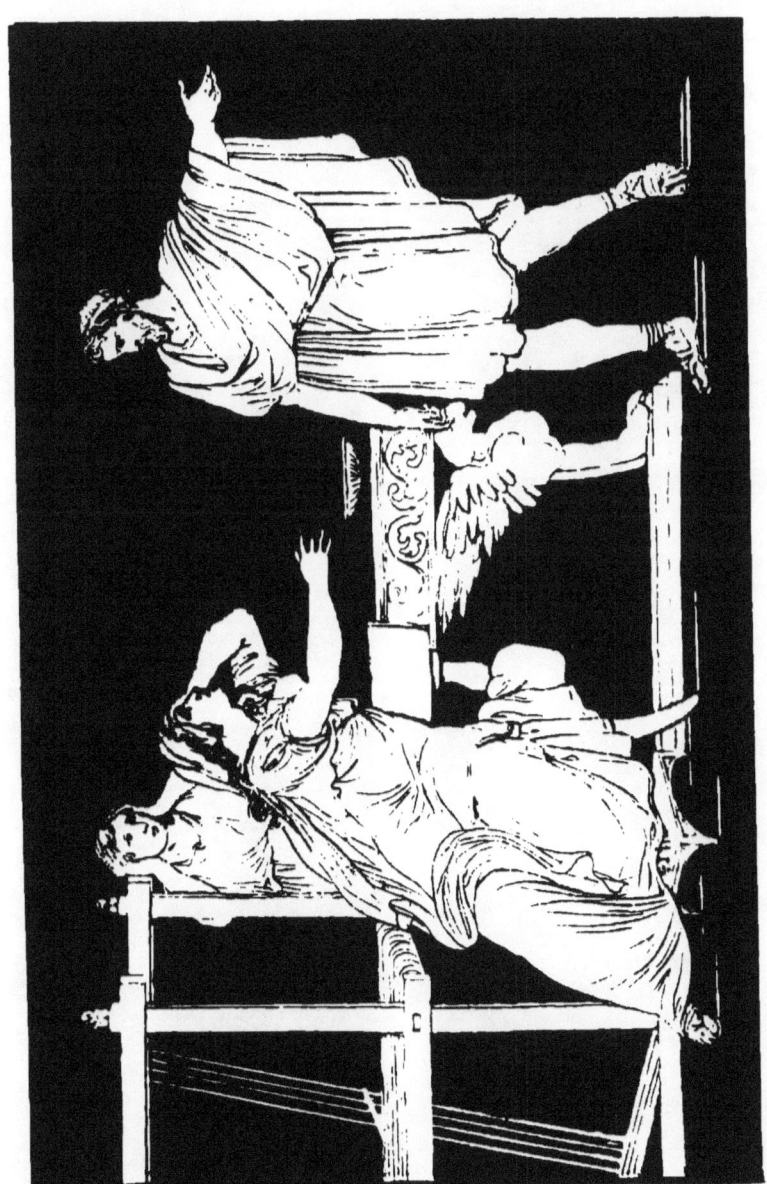

THE MOTHER OF EURYALUS RECEIVING THE NEWS OF HIS DEATH

But when with her wailing she touched the hearts of the men so that they forgat their valour, Ilioneus and Iülus commanded Idæus and Actor that they should lay hands upon her and carry her to her dwelling.

CHAPTER XXI.

THE BATTLE AT THE CAMP.

AND now the trumpet gave the signal for battle. First the Volscians drew near to the wall. These held their shields over their heads, joining them in close array so that they were like unto the shell of a tortoise, and they that bare them filled the moat and pulled down the wall. And some would have mounted the walls on ladders ; while the men of Troy cast spears at them and thrust at them with poles, being indeed well used to the manner of such a fight from walls. But on the covering of shields they threw down a huge block, breaking it through and scattering the men, who would not indeed fight any more in such fashion, but cast all manner of javelins and the like against the men of Troy. And Mezentius the Tuscan came on, shaking a lighted torch of pine in his hand, and Messapus tore down the rampart and called for a scaling-ladder, that he might mount up into the breach.

Now there was a tower upon the wall, which the Italians sought to take, and the men of Troy to defend it cast stones and darts through the loopholes thereof. On to this Turnus cast a torch, setting fire to the wall, and the flame, the wind fanning it, climbed from story to story. And when they that were therein fled to the part that was yet unconsumed, lo! the whole tower fell forward, and all perished, two only escaping, Helenor and Lycus. And Helenor was the elder, and when he saw that the enemy was about him on every side, then, even as a beast which the hunters compass about with a great ring waxeth desperate and flingeth himself over the nets upon their spears, so he threw himself on the ranks of the Latins where the spears were thickest, and so died. But Lycus was very swift of foot, and won even as far as the wall, and would fain have climbed thereon. But Turnus caught him, crying, " Thinkest thou to escape me?" and he laid hands upon him as he hung from the wall, dragging down much wall likewise : even as an eagle seizes a swan or a wolf a lamb, so he seized him. Then did the battle wax fiercer and fiercer, and many fell on this side and on that. For Ilioneus smote Lucetius when he would have set fire to the gates, and Capys slew Privernus, and Mezentius, having cast away his spear, smote the son of Arcens with a bullet of lead from his sling.

, And now Iülus, having used his bow aforetime on beasts of the field only, now first drew it against a man, even against Numanus, who had to wife the sister of Turnus. For this Numanus, thinking himself to be some great one, stood in the front rank, and defied the men of Troy, saying, "Are ye not ashamed, ye that have already been twice conquered, now to be besieged again ? What madness brought you to Italy ? We are a hardy race, for our new-born babes are dipped in the stream, and our boys are hunters in the woods ; and when we be men our hands are ever on the ploughshare or the sword, yea, and old age subdues us not, for when our hair is white yet do we cover it with the helmet. But ye with your mantles of purple and saffron, and sleeved tunics, and

ribboned mitres, lovers of sleep and of the
dance, ye men, nay rather ye women, of
Phrygia, what do ye here ? "

But the young Iülus endured not to hear such
boasting. He fixed an arrow in his bow and
drew the string, which was of horsehair, and ere
he let fly, he cried to Jupiter, " Help me now,
great Father, so will I bring, year by year, to
thy temple a steer with gilded horns." And
Jupiter heard, and thundered on the left hand.
And now, together with the thunder, clanged
the bow-string, sending death, and the arrow
hissed in the air and smote Numanus through
the head, even from temple to temple. " This
is the answer that the twice-conquered men of
Troy send thee." So cried the young Iülus,
and all the people shouted for joy. And Apollo,
where he sat in heaven and regarded the battle,
spake, " Go thou on as thou beginnest, child
and father of gods: 'tis thus that the race of
Troy shall hereafter bring all wars to an end."
Then he came down from heaven into the
camp of Troy, and took upon himself the shape
of the old man Butes : he had been aforetime
the armour-bearer of Anchises, and now fol-

lowed Iülus. And the god spake, saying, " It is enough that thou hast slain the boaster Numanus. The archer Apollo envieth thee not t his glory. But tempt the battle no more." So saying he vanished out of their sight. But the chiefs knew him who he was, yea, and heard the rattle of his quiver as he departed. And they suffered not Iülus to draw his bow again. But all the more the battle raged along the walls.

Now there were two youths, sons of Alcanor of Mount Ida, tall as pine-trees; and their names were Pandarus and Bitias. These having charge of the gate opened it, and standing on the right hand and on the left, even as towers, bade the enemy enter. And many of these, seeing the open gate, rushed forward, but fell slain upon the threshold. And now the men of Troy took heart, and pressed on beyond the walls.

But when Turnus heard tidings of these things he made haste to the gate. And first he slew Antiphates, who was a son of Sarpedon, and others also, and Bitias himself with them. Not with a javelin did he slay him (no javelin

had done such deed), but with a great spear of
Saguntum, having a point of a cubit's length.
Through two bulls' hides it passed and two
folds of his coat of mail. With a great crash
he fell, and his shield upon him, even as falls
a great pile which men set up in the bay of
Baiæ. So Bitias fell ; and Pandarus, his brother,
seeing that things fared ill with the men of
Troy, shut-to the gate, thrusting it into its
place with his broad shoulders. Many of his
companions he left without among their
enemies, and many he shut in. But being
blind with haste and fear, he saw not that he
shut in among them Prince Turnus himself.
But Turnus raged for blood, as a tiger rageth
among herds of cattle, and the men of Troy fled
before him. But Pandarus feared not to meet
him, hoping also that he should have vengeance for his brother. And he cried, " This is not
thy city of Ardea, but the camp of thy enemies.
Hence thou goest not forth." But Turnus
made answer, "Begin, if thou hast any valour in
thy heart. Thou shalt find another Achilles
here." Then Pandarus cast a great spear with
a knotted staff, whereon the bark was left ; but

Juno turned it aside, so that it fixed itself in the gate. And Turnus said, " My weapon thou escapest not thus, nor maketh my hand such error." And he lifted his sword, rising to the blow, and cleft the man's head, so that it fell divided upon his shoulders. Then, indeed, if only Turnus had bethought him to open the gate that the Latins should come in, there had come an end that day to the war and to the whole nation of Troy. But he thought not of it, caring only to slay the enemy. Many did he smite, some on the back as they fled, and some in front ; among them Amycus the hunter, and Clytius the singer, whom the Muses loved.

But now the chiefs of Troy, Mnestheus and Sergestus, began to gather the people together, and to make head against Turnus. And Mnestheus cried, "Whither will ye flee ? Have ye any walls beside ? Shall one man work such slaughter in the city ? Have you no thought, ye cowards, for your king ? " Then the men of Troy took heart again, and joined themselves in close array, so that Turnus could not but give way before them. Just so a lion is driven back by a crowd of men. Frightened is he, yet fierce withal, and his courage suffereth him not to flee, yet, so many are against him, he dareth not to stand. Even thus did Turnus give way. Twice he turned and put the men of Troy to flight, and twice they mastered him. For the helmet on his head rang with the javelins, and was broken with stones ; and the crest was stricken off, and the shield was shattered with blows ; and the sweat poured off from him, and scarce could he breathe, till at the last, having now come to the river, he plunged therein, and so returned to his companions.

And still the battle grew fiercer and fiercer about the walls, and the ring of them that defended the camp grew thinner and thinner. There stood Asius, the son of Imbrasus, and Clarus and Themon, brothers of Sarpedon the Lycian, and Acmon, the brother of Mnestheus, and others with them. And in the midst stood the young Iülus, with his comely head uncovered, like to a jewel that is set in gold or ivory, or that is compassed about with boxwood or terebinth.

15

CHAPTER XXII.

In the meanwhile Æneas had made alliance with Tarchon and the Tuscans. For when he had expounded all things to Tarchon their chief, telling him withal whence he had come, the people, believing that all things were now fulfilled as the Gods would have them, followed him willingly. Now, therefore, he was returning to the camp, leading the way in his ship, on the prow whereof were two lions, and above them the image of the goddess Ida. Pallas also sat beside him, and asked him, now concerning the stars by which men guide their ways at night, and now concerning the things which he had himself endured by land and sea.

After him came Massicus, in the Tiger, with whom were a thousand men from Clusium and Cosæ; and Abas, with six hundred from Populonia; and from Ilva, rich in mines, three hundred more. Asilas also, the soothsayer, came leading a thousand men from Pisa; and Astyr, the fairest of men, with three hundred from Cære and from the corn-fields of Minio and from Pyrgi.

Also the Ligurians came, with Cinyras, son of Cycnus, who had for his crest swan feathers; and his ship was called the Centaur. And Ocnus came from Mantua in the Mincius, and five hundred with him; and Aulestes in the Triton; and the number of the ships was thirty in all.

And now the night had fallen, and as Æneas sat at the helm, for care suffered him not to sleep, lo! there appeared to him a troop of Nymphs, which once had been his ships. And one of these, by name Cymodocea, came behind and caught the stern of the ship with her right hand, swimming meanwhile with the left. Then she spake, saying, "Wakest thou, son of the goddess? We are pines of Mount Ida, once thy ships, but now changed to Nymphs when Turnus would have burned us with fire. Know that thy son is besieged in the camp. Arm thyself therefore with the arms which Vulcan hath

wrought for thee.   To-morrow thou shalt lay
many Latins low in death."   And as she spake
she pushed the ship with her hand, and it
sped along through the waters and the rest
also with it.

And when the day was come, Æneas commanded that all should make them ready for
battle.   And now the camp was in his sight, as
he stood on the stern and lifted in his left hand
a flashing shield.   Much did the men of Troy
rejoice to see that sight, and shouted amain.
And Turnus and his companions marvelled, till
they looked behind them, and lo! the sea was
covered with ships, and in the midst was Æneas.
And it was as if a flame poured forth from his
helmet and his shield, bright as is a comet when
itshines in the night-time red as blood, or as
the Dog Star in the hot summer-tide with baleful light bringing fevers to the race of men.

Yet did not Turnus lose heart, but would
occupy the shore, and hinder from landing
those that came.   Wherefore he cried, " Now
have ye that which ye wished for.   Lo! the
enemy hides not himself behind a wall, but
meets us face to face.   Remember wife and

child and home and the great deeds of your fathers. Let us meet them on the shore ere yet their footing is firm." And he thought within himself who should watch the walls, and who should meet the enemy when he would gain the shore.

But in the meanwhile Æneas landed his men on gangways from the ships. And some leapt on shore, having watched for the ebb of the waves, and some ran along the oars. Tarchon also, the Etrurian, having spied a place where the sea broke not in waves, commanded his men that they should beach the ships. Which indeed they did without harm. Only the ship of Tarchon himself was caught upon a ridge and the men thrown therefrom. Yet these also, after a while, got safe to the shore.

Then did Æneas do great deeds against the enemy. For first he slew Theron, who surpassed all men in stature, smiting through his coat of mail; and Cisseus and Gyas, who wielded clubs after the manner of Hercules. Sons were they of Melampus, who had borne Hercules company in all his labours. Then the sons of Phorcus came against him, seven in number; and they

cast at him seven spears, whereof some re-
bounded from his shield and some grazed his
body, but harmed him not.   Then cried Æneas
to Achates, " Give me spears enough.   Spears
which have slain the Greeks on the fields of
Troy shall not be cast in vain against these
Latins."   Then of the seven he slew Mæon and
Alcanor, for the spear pierced the breast-plate
and heart of Mæon, and when Alcanor would
have held him up, passed through his arm and
yet kept on its way.   And many others fell on
this side and on that, for they fought with equal
fortune.   On the very threshold of Italy they
fought, and neither would the Italians give place
nor yet the men of Troy, for foot was planted
close to foot, and man stood fast by man.

In another part of the battle Pallas fought
with his Arcadians.   And when he saw that
they fled, not being wont to fight on foot (for
by reason of the ground they had sent away
their horses), he cried, " Now, by the name of
your King Evander, and by my hope that I may
win praise like unto his, I beseech you that ye
trust not to your feet.   Ye must make your way
through the enemy with your swords.   Where

the crowd is the thickest follow me. Nor have ye now gods against you. These are but mortal men that ye see." And he rushed into the midst of the enemy. First he smote Lagus with his spear, even as he was lifting a great stone from the earth. In the back he smote him, and, having smitten him, strove to draw forth the spear, and while he strove, Hisbo would have slain him; but Pallas was aware of his coming, and pierced him in the breast with his sword. Next he slew the twin brothers, Larides and Thymber. Very like they were, and it pleased father and mother that they knew not the one from the other; but Pallas made a cruel difference between them, for from Thymber he struck off the head, and from Larides the right hand. And after these he slew Rhœtus, as he fled past him in his chariot. And now, even as a shepherd sets fire to a wood, and the flames are borne along by the wind, so Pallas, and his Arcadians following, raged through the battle. And when Halæsus, the companion of Agamemnon, would have stayed them, Pallas, first praying to Father Tiber, smote him through the breast with a spear, that he died. Then came to the help of the Latins Lausus, the son of King Mezentius, and slew Abas of Populonia, and others also. Then the battle was equal for a space, for Pallas supported it on the one side and Lausus on the other. Fair were they both to behold and of equal age, and for both it was ordained that they should not return to their native country. Yet they met not in battle, seeing that the doom of each was that he should fall by a greater hand.

And now the nymph Juturna, who was sister to Turnus, bade her brother haste to the help of Lausus. And when he was come, he cried to the Latins, "Give place : I only will deal with Pallas. I only would that his father were here to see." Much did Pallas marvel to behold him and to see the men give place. But, being no whit afraid, he went forth into the space between the hosts, and the blood of the Arcadians ran cold when they saw him go. Then Turnus leapt from his chariot, for he would meet him on foot. And first Pallas prayed, saying, "O Hercules! if thou wast indeed my father's guest, help me to-day!" And Hercules heard him where he sat in heaven, and wept because he could avail nothing. Then said Father Jupiter, " My son, the days of men are numbered ; yet may they live for ever by noble deeds. This at least can valour do. Did not many sons of the gods fall at Troy ? yea, and my own Sarpedon. And for Turnus, too, the day of doom is at hand." And he turned his eyes from the battle. Then Pallas cast his spear with all his might. Through the shield of Turnus it passed, and through the corslet, yea, and grazed the top of his shoulder. Then Turnus balanced his spear awhile, and said, " This, methinks, shall better make its way," and he cast it. Through the shield, through the stout bull's hide, and through the folds of bronze it passed, and through the corslet, and pierced the breast of Pallas from front to back. And Pallas tore from the wound the reeking steel, and the blood gushed out, and the life therewith. Then Turnus stood above the corpse, and said, " Men of Arcadia, tell these my words to Evander : ' Pallas I send him back, even as he deserved that I should send him. I grudge him not due honours of burial. Yet of a truth the friendship of Æneas hath cost him

dear.'" Then he put his foot upon the body
and dragged therefrom the belt. Great and
heavy it was, and Clonius had wrought thereon in gold the deed of the fifty daughters of
Danaüs, how they slew their husbands in one
night. But even then the time was very near
when Turnus would wish that he had left that
spoil untouched. And afterwards, with much
groaning and weeping, the companions of Pallas
laid him upon a shield and bare him back.

And now tidings came to Æneas that it
fared ill with his men, and that Pallas was slain.
Across the field he sped, and all his heart was
full of wrath against Turnus and pity for the
old man Evander ; and first he took alive eight
youths, whom he should slay upon the tomb.
Then he cast his spear at Lagus ; but Lagus
avoided it by craft, and rushed forward, and
caught him by the knees, beseeching him by
the spirit of his father and the hopes of Iülus
that he would spare him, and take a ransom for
his life. But Æneas made answer, " Talk not
of sparing nor of ransom ; for to all courtesy of
war there is an end now that Turnus hath slain
Pallas." And he caught the man's helmet with

his left hand, and, bending back his neck, thrust
in the sword up to the hilt. And many other
valiant chiefs he slew, as Haemonides, priest of
Phœbus and Diana, and Tarquitus, son of
Faunus, and dark Camers, son of Volscens.
And now there met him two brethren on one
chariot, Lucagus and Liger. And Liger, who
indeed drave the horses, cried aloud, " These
are not the horses of Diomed, nor this the
chariot of Achilles, from which thou mayest
escape. Lo! the end of thy battles and thy
life is come." But Æneas spake not, but cast
his spear, and even as Lucagus made himself
ready for battle it sped through his shield and
pierced his thigh. Then he fell dying on the
plain. And Æneas cried, mocking him, " Thy
horses are not slow to flee, nor frightened by
a shadow. Of thine own will thou leavest thy
chariot." And he caught the horses by the
head. Then Liger stretched out his hands to
him in supplication, saying, " I beseech thee, by
thy parents, have pity upon me." But Æneas
made answer, " Nay, but thou spakest not thus
before. Die! and desert not thy brother." And
he thrust the sword into his breast. Thus did

Æneas deal death through the host, even as he had been the giant Typhoeus with the hundred hands. And when Iülus and the men of Troy beheld him they broke forth from the camp.

And now Juno bethought her how she might save Turnus, whom she loved. So she caused that there should pass before his eyes an image as of Æneas, which seemed to defy him to battle. And when Turnus would have fought, lo! the false Æneas fled, and Turnus followed him. Now there chanced to be lying moored to a great rock a certain ship, on which King Asinius had come from Clusium. Into this the false Æneas fled, and Turnus followed hard upon him, but found not the man. And when he looked, Juno had burst the moorings of the ship, and the sea was about him on every side. Then he cried, "What have I done, great Jupiter, that I should suffer such shame? What think the Latins of my flight? Drown me, ye winds and waves, or drive me where no man may see me more." Thrice he would have cast himself into the sea; thrice would he have slain himself with the sword; but Juno

forbad, and brought him safe to the city of
Daunus, his father.

In the meanwhile King Mezentius joined
the battle. Nor could the men of Troy, nor
yet the Tuscans, stay him. Many valiant men
he slew, as Mimas, whom his mother Theano
bare the same night that Hecuba bare Paris to
King Priam ; and Actor, a Greek, who had left
his promised wife, and carried her purple favour
in his helmet ; and tall Orodes. Orodes, indeed,
was flying, but the king deigned not to slay
him in his flight, but met him face to face and
smote him. Also when Orodes cried, " Whoever thou art, thou goest not long unpunished :
a like doom awaits thee ; and in this land shalt
thou find thy grave," Mezentius laughed, and
made answer, " Die thou, but let the king
of Gods and men see to me."

But after awhile Æneas spied Mezentius as
he fought, and made haste to meet him. Nor
did the king give place, but cried, " Now may
this right hand and the spear which I wield be
my gods, and help me." And he cast his spear.
It smote the shield of Æneas, but pierced it
not. Yet did it not fly in vain, for glancing

off it smote Antores in the side—Antores who once had been comrade to Hercules, and afterwards followed Evander. Now he fell, and in his death remembered the city which he loved, even Argos. Then in his turn Æneas cast his spear. Through the bull's-hide shield it passed, wounding the king in the groin, but not to death. And Æneas was right glad to see the blood flow forth, and drew his sword and pressed on; and Mezentius, much cumbered with the spear and the wound, gave place. But when Lausus, his son, saw this, he groaned aloud and leapt forward, and took the blow upon his sword; and his companions followed him with a shout, and cast their spears at Æneas, staying him till Mezentius had gotten himself safe away. And Æneas stood awhile under the shower of spears, even as a traveller stands hiding himself from a storm. Then he cried to Lausus, "What seekest thou, madman? Why venturest thou that which thy strength may not endure?" But Lausus heeded him not at all, but still pressed on. Then the heart of Æneas was filled with wrath, and the day was come for Lausus that he should die. For the king smote him

ÆNEAS AND THE BODY OF LAUSUS.

with his sword : through shield it passed and tunic woven with gold, and was hidden to the hilt in his body. And Æneas pitied him as he lay dead, bethinking him how he, too, would fain have died for his father, and spake, saying, "What shall Æneas give thee, unhappy boy, for this thy nobleness ? Keep thy arms, in which thou hadst such delight, and let thy father care as he will for thy body ; and take this comfort in thy death, that thou fallest by the hand of the great Æneas." Then he lifted him from the earth, and bade his companions carry him away.

In the mean time his father tended his wounds, leaning on the trunk of a tree by the Tiber bank. His helmet hung from a branch, and his arms lay upon the ground, while his followers stood around. And ever he asked tidings of Lausus, and sent those who should bid him return. But when they brought back his body on a shield, his father knew it from afar, and threw dust upon his white hair, and fell upon the body, crying, " Had I such desire to live, my son, that I suffered thee to meet in my stead the sword of the enemy ? Am I saved by these wounds? Do I live by thy death? And indeed, my son, I did dishonour to thee by my misdeeds. Would that I had given my guilty life for thine! But indeed I die; nevertheless not yet, for I have first some-what that I must do."

Then he raised himself on his thigh, and commanded that they should bring his horse. His pride it was and comfort, and had borne him conqueror from many fights. Very sad was the beast, and he spake to it, saying, "O Rhœbus, thou and I have lived long enough, if indeed aught on earth be long. To-day thou shalt bring back the head and the arms of Æneas, and so avenge my Lausus; or thou shalt die with me. For a Trojan master thou wilt not, I know, endure."

Then he mounted the horse and took spears in both his hands, and so hasted to meet Æneas. Thrice he called him by name, and Æneas rejoiced to hear his voice, and cried, " Now may Jupiter and Apollo grant that this be true. Begin the fight." And Mezentius made answer: " Seek not to make afraid. Thou canst do me no harm now that thou hast

slain my son. I am come to die, but take thou
first this gift;" and he cast his spear, and then
another, and yet another, as he rode in a great
circle about the enemy. But they brake not
the boss of gold. And Æneas stood firm,
bearing the forest of spears in his shield. But
at last, issuing forth in anger from behind his
shield, he cast his spear and smote the war-horse
Rhœbus between his temples. Then the horse
reared himself and lashed the air with his feet,
and fell with his rider beneath him. And the men
of Troy and the Latins sent up a great shout.
Then Æneas hasted and drew his sword, and
stood above him, crying, "Where is the fierce
Mezentius now?" And the king said, when he
breathed again, "Why threatenest thou me
with death? Slay me; thou wrongest me not.
I made no covenant with thee for life, nor did
my Lausus when he died for me. Yet grant
me this one thing. Thou knowest how my
people hateth me. Keep my body, I pray
thee, from them, that they do it no wrong.
And let my son be buried with me in my
grave." And he gave his throat to the sword,
and feared not.

16

CHAPTER XXIII.

THE COUNCIL.

So the battle had an end. And the next day, early in the morning, Æneas paid his vows. For he took an oak - tree, and lopped the branches round about, and set it on a mound. And thereon he hung, for a trophy to Mars, the arms of King Mezentius, the crest dripping with blood, and the headless spears, and the corslet pierced in twelve places. Also he fastened on the left hand the shield, and hung about the neck the ivory-hilted sword. And next, the chiefs being gathered about him, he spake, saying, " We have wrought a great deed. Here ye see all that remaineth of Mezentius. Now, therefore, let us make ready to carry the war against the city of Latinus. This, therefore, will we do with the first light to-morrow. And now let us bury the dead, doing such honour to them as we may, for indeed

they have purchased a country for us with
their own blood. But first will I send back
Pallas to the city of Evander."

Then he went to the tent where the dead
body was laid, and old Accœtes kept watch
thereby—Accœtes, who had been armour-bearer
to Evander, and now had followed his son, but
with evil fortune ; and the women of Troy, with
their hair unbound, mourned about him. But
when they saw Æneas they beat their breasts,
and sent up a great cry even to heaven. And
when the king saw the pillowed head and the
great wound in the breast he wept, and said,
"Ah! why did Fortune grudge me this, that
thou shouldst see my kingdom, and go back in
triumph to thy father's home? This is not
what I promised to Evander when he gave
thee to my charge, and warned me that the
men of Italy were valiant and fierce. And now
haply, old man, thou makest offerings and prayers
for him who now hath no part nor lot in the
Gods of heaven. Yet, at least, thou wilt see
that he beareth an honourable wound. But
what a son thou losest, O Italy! and what a
friend, thou, Iülus!"

Then he chose a thousand men who should go with the dead and share the father's grief. After this they made a bier of arbutus boughs and oak, and put also over it a canopy of branches, and laid the dead thereon, like unto a flower of violet or hyacinth which a girl hath plucked, which still hath beauty and colour, but the earth nourisheth it no more. And Æneas took two robes of purple, which Dido had woven with thread of gold, and with one he wrapped the body and with the other the head. And behind were carried the arms which Pallas had won in fight ; and they led the old man Acœtes, smiting on his breast and tearing his cheeks, and throwing himself upon the ground ; and the war-horse Æthon walked beside, with the great tears rolling down his cheeks. And also they bare behind him his helmet and shield, for all else Turnus had taken ; and then followed the whole company, the men of Troy, the Arcadians, and the Tuscans, with arms reversed. And Æneas said, " The same cares and sorrows of war call me elsewhere. Farewell, my Pallas, for ever !" And he departed to the camp.

And now there came ambassadors from the

city, having olive-branches about their heads, praying for a truce, that they might bury their dead. Then Æneas made answer, " Ye ask peace for the dead ; fain would I give it to the living. I had not come to this land but for the bidding of the Fates. And if your king changeth from me and my friendship to Turnus, I am blameless. Yet methinks Turnus should rather have taken this danger upon himself. And even now, if he be willing to fight with me, man to man, so be it. But now bury ye your dead."

Then they made a truce for twelve days. And the men of Troy and the Latins laboured together, hewing wood upon the hills, pine and cedar and mountain ash. And the men of Troy built great piles upon the shore and burned the dead bodies of their companions thereon, and their arms with them. And the Latins did likewise. Also they that had been chosen to do this thing carried the body of Pallas to his city. And King Evander and the Arcadians made a great mourning for him.

But when they had made an end of burning the dead there arose a great tumult in the city, for many had lost husband, or brother, or son.

Wherefore they cried out that it was an evil war, and they cursed the marriage of Turnus, and would have him fight with Æneas, man to man, that there might be an end of these troubles. And lo! in the midst of the tumult there came back the ambassadors that had been sent to Diomed, saying that their prayers and gifts had availed nothing. Then King Latinus called a council of the chiefs, and sat him down upon his throne, and bade the men say on. Then Venulus, who was the chiefest among them, spake, saying, "We went to Arpi, to the city of King Diomed. And the man received us, and asked us wherefore we had come, and when we had told him, he spake, saying, "Men of Italy, why will ye thus tempt your fate? Know ye not that we, as many of us as lifted hand against the men of Troy, have suffered grievous things? For the Lesser Ajax perished on the rocks of Eubœa; and Menelaüs was driven even to the island of Proteus, which is hard by the land of Egypt; and Ulysses scarcely escaped from the Cyclops; and as for King Agamemnon, an adulterer slew him in his palace. And us the Gods suffered not to see wife or country again.

But as for this which ye ask of me, I fight not against men of Troy any more. These gifts which ye bring to me, give rather to Æneas. We have fought together, and I know how mightily he rises to the stroke of his sword and casts his spear. I tell you this: if there had been in Troy two others such as he, the war had come to the gates of Argos, and Greece had suffered even what she wrought. 'Twas he and Hector who for ten years bore up against our arms: both valiant men and strong, and this man the dearer to the Gods. Make peace with him, if ye may; but beware that ye meet him not in war."

And when they had made an end of speaking, there was a murmur in the council, some saying one thing, and some another. Then King Latinus said from his throne, " This is an ill time for counsel when the enemy is about our walls. Yet hearken to my words. Ye do ill to wage this war: for the men of Troy are dear to the Gods, nor may any sword prevail against them. Ye have heard what saith King Diomed; ye see also how low our fortunes be brought. My sentence therefore is this: I have a domain

near to the Tiber, stretching far to the west, a
land of corn-fields and pasture.   This, and the
pine forests also on the hills, will I give to the
men of Troy, and I will divide also my kingdom.
But if they would rather seek some other land,
let us build them twelve ships, or more, if they
be able to fill them, and let them depart in peace.
Now therefore let us send ambassadors, even a
hundred men, and let them carry gifts, talents of
gold, and ivory, and also a throne and a robe
which are the emblems of kingship."

Then spake Drances.   (Now Drances had
great jealousy of Turnus.   Bountiful was he,
and eloquent, and skilful in counsel and debate,
but feeble in fight.)   " This matter about which
thou askest us, O King, is manifest, and needeth
not speech ; for all men know what shall best
profit the people, yet fear to say it.   'Tis this
man that hindereth us from speech ; this man
for whose evil pride—aye, I will say it though
he threaten me with death—so many valiant
chiefs have fallen, while he makes a vain show
of his valour.   And now, O King, I would bid
thee add one more to thy gifts.   Give thy
daughter to this great son-in-law, and make

peace sure for ever. Yea, Turnus, yield thou
this to thy country. Lo! we all ask it of thee,
even I, whom thou holdest to be thine enemy.
But if thou wilt not, counting a royal wife to be
more than thy country, call not on us to die for
thee, but meet thy rival face to face."

Then in great wrath Turnus made answer,
"Thou hast always many words at command,
O Drances, and, when the senators are called,
art ever the first to come. But where is thy
valour? Where are the trophies which thy
right hand hath set up? Wilt thou make trial
of it now? Lo! the enemy is at hand. Shall
we go? Dost thou linger? Is all thy valour
in thy boasting tongue and coward feet? And
thou doubtest, forsooth, of my courage. What?
hast thou not heard of Pallas slain, and Bitias
and Pandarus, and all whom I laid low when
they shut me within their walls? And now I
would speak of thee and thy counsel, my father.
If thou thinkest that one defeat is enough, and
that fortune may not change, be it so: let us
pray for peace. Happy then he who hath died
before he saw such foul disgrace! But if we
have yet strength remaining, and nations and

cities that will yet help us ; if these men of
Troy have won their victory dear, why faint we
at the threshold, and tremble before the trumpet
sounds ? Diomed will not help us. But we have
Messapus, and the augur Tolumnius, and all the
chiefs of Italy, yea and the Volscian Camilla,
with her squadrons clad in bronze. And if
they would have me fight man to man, I refuse
not in such a cause. Let him be mighty as
Achilles, and don the arms which Vulcan hath
made.   I refuse not the battle, for my life is for
you and for your king."

But while they disputed there came a messenger unto the palace bringing tidings of fear.
For the men of Troy, he said, were marching
in battle line from their camp. Then there
arose a great uproar, some crying aloud for arms,
and some weeping ; loud was it as the clamour
of birds that settle in some deep wood, or of
swans by the mouth of Po. And Turnus cried,
"Call your councils, my friends, speak of peace
as you sit. But the enemy is at the gate."
And he made haste and rushed forth from the
senate-house.

CHAPTER XXIV.

THEN Turnus commanded that of the chiefs some should set the battle in array, and some should fortify the gates, and some should follow after himself. And men dug trenches before the gates, and gathered store of stones and stakes; and the women and children stood upon the walls. But the queen and the chiefest of the matrons went to the temple of Pallas, and with them was the virgin Lavinia, from whom all these sorrows sprang, casting down her beautiful eyes to the ground. And they offered incense and prayer to the goddess, that she would break the Phrygian robber's spear, and lay him low before the walls of the city. Then Turnus armed himself for the battle, and ran down from the citadel, and lo! at the gate there met him Camilla, with a troop of virgins riding on horses. And when they had lighted down therefrom, the Queen spake, saying, " I promise thee, Turnus, to meet the horsemen of Troy and of the Tuscans. Do thou abide here on foot and guard the walls." And Turnus, steadfastly regarding her, made answer, " What thanks shall I give thee for such service? But now hearken to me. There lieth a valley whereby Æneas purposeth to come against this city : in the mouth thereof will I lay an ambush ; do thou, therefore, meet the Tuscan horsemen in battle, having with thee Messapus and the horsemen of Tibur." And when he had said this he departed and laid the ambush against Æneas.

In the mean time Diana, where she sat in heaven, spake to Opis, who was one of the nymphs that waited on her : "Camilla goeth forth to battle, who is dearer to me than all virgins beside, and hath been so even from a child. She is the daughter of King Metabus. Now Metabus, being banished from his city, even Privernum, by reason of his violence, fled, taking with him his daughter. Her he carried in his bosom, and the Volscians pressed hard upon him as he fled. And he came to the

river Amasenus, and it chanced that the river
was swollen with abundance of rain, and over-
flowed his banks. And the king, when he
would have crossed it by swimming, feared for
the child. Therefore he took the great spear
which he carried in his hand, and bound the
girl thereto with strips of bark, and balanced it
in his hands, saying, " I vow this child to thee,
daughter of Latona, to be thy servant for ever."
And he cast the spear with all his might, so
that it fell on the other side of the river. Then
did he throw himself into the stream, and so
escaped from the land of his enemies. Thereafter he dwelt not in house or city, but lived on
the hills with the shepherds. And the child he
nourished with mare's milk, and the like. And
when she could first put her feet upon the ground,
he put a javelin in her hand, and gave her a
bow also and arrows. No gold had she on her
hair, nor wore she long garments such as women
use, but was adorned with a tiger-skin. Also
from a child she would cast the javelin from her
hand, and whirl the sling above her head, and
strike the crane or the wild swan even in the
midst of the clouds. Many Tuscan mothers

would have had her for their daughter-in-law, but marriage pleased her not. I would she had not come to this war. Then had I made her one of my companions. But seeing that her doom is upon her, I give thee this charge concerning her. Pass thou down to the earth, to the Latin land, where they begin even now this evil battle. And take from thy quiver an avenging arrow, and whosoever shall harm the virgin, be he man of Troy or Italian, shall pay the penalty. But her will I carry back to her native country, neither shall any man spoil her of her arms."

In the meanwhile Æneas and his army were come near to the walls. And first the horsemen ran together against each other, holding their spears forth in front. In this battle Tyrrhenus the Tuscan met Aconteus, and drave him from his horse with the shock, as a thunderbolt is driven from the sky or a stone from an engine; and the ranks of the Latins were troubled and fled, and the men of Troy pursued them; but when they came near to the gates the Latins turned upon them, and the men of Troy fled in their turn. Even as a wave upon the shore floweth and ebbeth, so twice they fled and twice they pursued. But the third time they joined battle, and gave not place one to the other. Then fell many men and horses dying to the ground. Orsilochus smote the horse of Remulus between the temples, and the beast reared and threw his rider to the earth. Next Catillus of Tibur slew Iollas, and Herminius, who fought with breast and shoulders bare, driving his spear through him from side to side. But fiercest of all was the virgin Camilla. With one breast bare she fought; and now she would shoot arrows from her bow, and now would ply the battle-axe. And the virgins that were her fellows, as Larina and Tulla and Tarpeia, followed close behind her. Like to the Amazons they were when, having their shields shaped as is the moon, they throng around their Queen Penthesilea or Hippolyté. Euneüs she slew, a man of Troy; and Pagasus and Liris, Etruscans; and others besides. With every arrow she slew a man. And the hunter Ornytus came against her, having for helmet the head of a wolf with white teeth, and in his hand a hunting spear. He was of greater stature than other men, but she slew him, and mocked him, saying, "Didst thou think, Tuscan, that thou wert hunting wild beasts this day? Lo! a woman's arms have brought thy boasts to nothing." Then she slew Orsilochus and Butes, mighty men of Troy. Butes she smote as he fled from her, but from Orsilochus she made as she would flee; then, wheeling round, met him face to face, and cleft his head in twain. The son of Aunus, whose father dwelt amongst the Apennines, trembled to see the deed, and was fain to escape her by craft, after the fashion of his country, being a man of Liguria. Therefore he said, "What glory is it if thou prevailest by reason of the swiftness of thy horse? Fight with me now on foot, and let us see who shall gain the victory." And when the virgin leapt to the ground, giving her horse to her companions, he turned his horse to flee. But the virgin cried, "Thinkest thou to escape me thus, thou fool? Never shalt thou see thy father, the crafty Aunus, again." And she made haste and outran the horse, and catching the reins in her hands, stood before him and slew him.

Then did Tarchon the Tuscan rebuke his

CAMILLA AND THE SON OF AUNUS.

horsemen, calling each by his name, and saying,
"What fear, what baseness, is this, ye Tuscans?
Shall a woman drive you before her? Ready
enough are ye for the dance, and the feast, and
the sacrifice; but ye lag behind in war." And
he drave his horse at Venulus of Tibur, and
caught him in his arms, and carried him away.
As an eagle carries a snake which he hath caught,
and the snake, winding his coils about the bird,
struggles and hisses, so did Tarchon carry him
off, and spy out a place where he might smite
him, and Venulus strove amain to keep the
sword from his throat. And all the men of
Troy and the Tuscans charged again when they
saw their chief do so valiantly.

But all the while Arruns watched the virgin
Camilla, that he might take her unawares. Now
there was a certain Chloreus, priest of Cybelé,
who rode through the battle, very splendid to behold. For his horse was clad in bronze mail, that
was clasped with gold; and he himself was clad
in purple from beyond the seas; his bow was
of Lycia and his arrows of Crete; of gold was
his bow, and of gold the helmet; and his saffron
scarf was clasped with gold; and his tunic was

17

embroidered with needlework, and his trews were of divers colours. Him alone the virgin followed, blind to all beside, with a woman's love of beautiful spoil. And Arruns watched her from the ambush where he lay; and when the time was come, he cried, " Apollo, lord of Soracte, help me now; if ever I and my people have passed over the burning coals in thy honour, help me now. I seek not spoil nor glory; let me return without honour to my country, so but I slay this fury." And part of his prayer the god heard, and part was scattered by the winds. Camilla, indeed, he slew, but to his country he went not back. But when the bow twanged, all the Volscians turned their eyes to the queen; but she was not aware of the arrow, even till it smote her under her breast. Then her companions ran together and caught her as she fell. And she would have drawn forth the arrow, but it was deep in her side. Then did her eyes swim cold in death, and the colour, that was as the colour of a rose, faded from her cheek. And as she died, she said to Acca, who was dearest to her of all her companions, "Acca, my sister, my strength faileth

THE DEATH OF CAMILLA

me. Bid Turnus that he join the battle, and keep the men of Troy from the city." And she loosed hold of the reins, and fell to the earth; and the battle grew fiercer as she lay.

But when the nymph Opis saw that she was dead, she groaned, and cried, " O Virgin, thou hast paid the penalty of thy deed, in that thou defiedst the men of Troy. Neither hath it profited thee to be the servant of Diana. Yet will she not have thee unhonoured in thy death; for whosoever hath harmed thee shall surely die." Then she flew through the air, and lighted on a mound that was the tomb of Laurens, that had once been king of the land. And when she saw Arruns boasting of his deed—for at first he had fled stricken with fear, but had now taken heart again — she cried, " Come hither, that thou mayest suffer thy doom, in that thou hast slain the virgin Camilla." And she drew the bow till the ends thereof came close together, and her left hand was on the arrow-head and her right hand on the string. And even as Arruns heard the clang of the bow the arrow smote him that he died.

But when Camilla was dead her companions

fled, and the Rutulians also, and the chiefs were scattered and the battalions left desolate. And there rose a great cloud of dust that rolled ever nearer the city; and a dreadful shout went up to heaven. Then those that first came to the gates were trodden down by the crowd behind them, that they died, yea, even in the sight of their homes. And those that were within shut the gates and drave back with arms such as would have entered. And then was slaughter and confusion without end. And even the women upon the walls cast javelins with their hands, and thrust with stakes of wood that had been charred with fire, even as with spears.

But now there came ill tidings to Turnus as he lay in ambush in the wood, even that Camilla was dead, and that the enemy had the mastery. Wherefore he rose up from his place, and came out upon the plain; and even as he rose up, Æneas had won his way through the wood and overpassed the ridge. Then did they both haste towards the walls. And Æneas saw Turnus, and knew him, and Turnus also saw Æneas; but the darkness hindered them that they should not fight together that day.

CHAPTER XXV.

THE BROKEN TREATY.

PRINCE TURNUS, seeing that the Latins had fled in the battle, and that men looked to him that he should perform that which he had promised, even to meet Æneas face to face, was filled with rage. Even as a lion which a hunter hath wounded breaketh the arrow wherewith he hath been stricken, and rouseth himself to battle, shaking his mane and roaring, so Turnus arose. And first he spake to King Latinus, saying, "Not for me, my father, shall these cowards of Troy go back from that which they have covenanted. I will meet this man face to face, and slay him while ye look on ; or, if the Gods will that he vanquish me so, he shall rule over you, and have Lavinia to wife."

But King Latinus made answer : " Yet think awhile, my son. Thou hast the kingdom of thy father Daunus ; and there are other noble

virgins in Latium whom thou mayest have to
wife. Wilt thou not then be content? For to
give my daughter to any husband of this nation
I was forbidden, as thou knowest. Yet did I
disobey, being moved by love of thee, my wife
also beseeching me with many tears. Thou seest
what troubles I and my people, and thou more
than all, have suffered from that time. Twice
have we fled in the battle, and now the city
only is left to us. If I must yield me to these
men, let me yield whilst thou art yet alive.
For what doth it profit me that thou shouldst
die? Nay, but all men would cry shame on
me if I gave thee to death!"

Now for a space Turnus spake not for wrath.
Then he said, " Be not troubled for me, my
father. For I, too, can smite with the spear;
and as for this Æneas, his mother will not be
at hand to snatch him in a cloud from my
sight."

Then Amata cried to him, saying, " Fight
not, I, beseech thee, with these men of Troy,
my son; for surely what thou sufferest I also
shall suffer. Nor will I live to see Æneas my
son-in-law."

And Lavinia heard the voice of her mother, and wept. As a man stains ivory with crimson, or as roses are seen mixed with lilies, even so the virgin's face burned with crimson. And Turnus, regarding her, loved her exceedingly, and made answer: " Trouble me not with tear or idle words, my mother, for to this battle I must go. And do thou, Idmon the herald, say to the Phrygian king, " To-morrow, when the sun shall rise, let the people have peace, but we two will fight together. And let him that prevaileth have Lavinia to wife."

Then first he went to the stalls of his horses. The wife of the North Wind gave them to Pilumnus. Whiter than snow were they, and swifter than the wind. Then he put the coat of mail about his shoulders, and fitted a helmet on his head, and took the great sword which Vulcan had made for Daunus his father, and had dipped it when it was white-hot in the river of Styx. His spear also he took where it stood against a pillar, saying, " Serve me well, my spear, that hast never failed me before, that I may lay low this womanish robber of Phrygia, and soil with dust his curled and perfumed hair."

The next day the men of Italy and the men
of Troy measured out a space for the battle.
And in the midst they builded an altar of turf.
And the two armies sat on the one side and on
the other, having fixed their spears in the earth
and laid down their shields. Also the women
and the old men stood on the towers and roofs
of the city, that they might see the fight.

But Queen Juno spake to Juturna, the sister
of Turnus, saying, "Seest thou how these two are
now about to fight, face to face? And indeed
Turnus goeth to his death. As for me, I endure
not to look upon this covenant or this battle.
But if thou canst do aught for thy brother, lo!
the time is at hand." And when the Nymph
wept and beat her breast, Juno said, " This is
no time for tears. Save thy brother, if thou
canst, from death; or cause that they break this
covenant."

After this came the kings, that they might
make the covenant together. And King
Latinus rode in a chariot with four horses, and
he had on his head a crown with twelve rays
of gold, for he was of the race of the Sun; and
Turnus came in a chariot with two white

horses, having a javelin in either hand ; and
Æneas had donned the arms which Vulcan had
made, and with him was the young Iülus. And
after due offering Æneas sware, calling on all
the Gods, " If the victory shall fall this day to
Turnus, the men of Troy shall depart to the
city of Evander, nor trouble this land any more.
But if it fall to me, I will not that the Latins
should serve the men of Troy. Let the nations
be equal one with the other. The gods that
I bring we will worship together, but King
Latinus shall reign as before. A new city
shall the men of Troy build for me, and Lavinia
shall call it after her own name."

Then King Latinus sware, calling on the
Gods that are above and the Gods that are
below, saying, " This covenant shall stand for
ever, whatsoever may befall. As sure as this
sceptre which I bear—once it was a tree, but a
cunning workman closed it in bronze, to be the
glory of Latium's kings—shall never again bear
twig or leaf, so surely shall this covenant be
kept."

But the thing pleased not the Latins ; for
before, indeed, they judged that the battle

would not be equal between the two; and now
were they the more assured, seeing them when
they came together, and that Turnus walked
with eyes cast to the ground, and was pale and
wan. Wherefore there arose a murmuring among
the people, which when Juturna perceived, she
took upon herself the likeness of Camers, who
was a prince and a great warrior among them,
and passed through the host, saying, " Are ye
not ashamed, men of Italy, that one man should
do battle for you all ? For count these men :
surely they are scarce one against two. And if
he be vanquished, what shame for you ! As for
him, indeed, though he die, yet shall his glory
reach to the heavens ; but ye shall suffer disgrace, serving these strangers for ever."

And when she saw that the people were
moved, she gave also a sign from heaven. For
lo! an eagle that drave a crowd of sea-fowl before him, swooped down to the water, and caught
a great swan ; and even while the Italians
looked, the birds that before had fled turned
and pursued the eagle, and drave him before
them, so that he dropped the swan and fled
away. Which thing when the Italians per-

ceived, they shouted, and made them ready for battle. And the augur Tolumnius cried, "This is the token that I have looked for. For this eagle is the stranger, and ye are the birds, which before, indeed, have fled, but shall now make him to flee."

And he ran forward and cast his spear, smiting a man of Arcadia below the belt, upon the groin. One of nine brothers was he, sons of a Tuscan mother, but their father was a Greek; and they, when they saw him slain, caught swords and spears, and ran forward. And straightway the battle was begun. First they brake down the altars, that they might take firebrands therefrom; and King Latinus fled from the place. Then did Messapus drive his horses against King Aulestes of Mantua, who, being fain to fly, stumbled upon the altar and fell headlong on the ground. And Messapus smote him with a spear that was like a weaver's beam, saying, "This, of a truth, is a worthier victim." After this Coryneüs the Arcadian, when Ebysus would have smitten him, snatched a brand from the altar and set fire to the beard of the man, and, before he came to himself, caught him by the hair, and thrusting him to the ground, so slew him. And when Podalirius pursued Alsus the shepherd, and now held his sword over him ready to strike, the other turned, and with a battle-axe cleft the man's head from forehead to chin.

But all the while the righteous Æneas, having his head bare, and holding neither spear nor sword, cried to the people, "What seek ye? what madness is this? The covenant is established, and I only have the right to do battle." But even while he spake an arrow smote him, wounding him. But who let it fly no man knoweth; for who, of a truth, would boast that he had wounded Æneas? And he departed from the battle.

CHAPTER XXVI.

THE DEATH OF TURNUS.

Now when Turnus saw that Æneas had departed from the battle he called for his chariot. And when he had mounted thereon he drave it through the host of the enemy, slaying many valiant heroes, as Sthenelus and Pholus, and the two sons of Imbrasus the Lycian, Glaucus and Lades. Then he saw Eumedes, son of that Dolon who would have spied out the camp of the Greeks, asking as his reward the horses of Achilles (but Diomed slew him). Him Turnus smote with a javelin from afar, and, when he fell, came near and put his foot upon him, and taking his sword drave it into his neck, saying, "Lo! now thou hast the land which thou soughtest. Lie there, and measure out Italy for thyself." Many others he slew, for the army fled before him. Yet did one man, Phegeus by name, stand against him, and would

have stayed the chariot, catching the bridles of
the horses in his hand.   But as he clung to the
yoke and was dragged along, Turnus broke
his cuirass with his spear, and wounded him.
And when the man set his shield before him,
and made at Turnus with his sword, the wheels
dashed him to the ground, and Turnus struck
him between the helmet and the breast-plate,
and smote off his head.

But in the meanwhile Mnestheus and Achates
and Iülus led Æneas to the camp, leaning on
his spear.   Very wrath was he, and strove to
draw forth the arrow.   And when he could not,
he commanded that they should open the wound
with the knife, and so send him back to the
battle.   Iapis also, the physician, ministered to
him.   Now this Iapis was dearer than all other
men to Apollo, and when the god would have
given him all his arts, even prophecy and music
and archery, he chose rather to know the virtues
of herbs and the art of healing, that so he might
prolong the life of his father, who was even
ready to die.   This Iapis, then, having his garments girt about him in healer's fashion, would
have drawn forth the arrow with the pincers,

but could not. And while he strove, the battle came nearer, and the sky was hidden by clouds of dust, and javelins fell thick into the camp. But when Venus saw how grievously her son was troubled, she brought from Ida, which is a mountain of Crete, the herb dittany. A hairy stalk it hath and a purple flower. The wild goats know it well if so be that they have been wounded by arrows. This, then, Venus, having hidden her face, brought and dipped into the water, and sprinkled there with ambrosia and sweet-smelling panacea.

And Iapis, unawares, applied the water that had been healed ; and lo ! the pain was stayed and the blood was staunched, and the arrow came forth, though no man drew it, and Æneas's strength came back to him as before. Then said Iapis, "Art of mine hath not healed thee, my son. The Gods call thee to thy work." Then did Æneas arm himself again, and when he had kissed Iülus and bidden him farewell, he went forth to the battle. And all the chiefs went with him, and the men of Troy took courage and drave back the Latins. Then befell a great slaughter, for Gyas slew Ufens, who was the leader of the Æquians; also Tolumnius, the great augur, was slain, who had first broken the covenant, slaying a man with his spear. But Æneas deigned not to turn his hand against any man, seeking only for Turnus, that he might fight with him. But when the nymph Juturna perceived this she was sore afraid. Therefore she came near to the chariot of her brother, and thrust out Metiscus, his charioteer, where he held the reins, and herself stood in his room, having made herself like to him in shape and voice. Then as a swallow flies through the halls and arcades of some rich man's house, seeking food for its young, so Juturna drave the chariot of her brother hither and thither. And ever Æneas followed behind, and called to him that he should stay; but whenever he espied the man, and would have overtaken him by running, then again did Juturna turn the horses about and flee. And as he sped Messapus cast a spear at him. But Æneas saw it coming, and put his shield over him, resting on his knee. Yet did the spear smite him on the helmet-top and shear off the crest. Then indeed was his wrath kindled, and he rushed into the army of the enemy, slaying many as he went.

Then was there a great slaughter made on this side and on that. But after a while Venus put it into the heart of Æneas that he should lead his army against the city. Therefore he called together the chiefs, and, standing in the midst of them on a mound, spake, saying, "Hearken now to my words, and delay not to fulfil them, for of a truth Jupiter is on our side. I am purposed this day to lay this city of Latinus even with the ground, if they still refuse to obey. For why should I wait for Turnus till it please him to meet me in battle?"

Then did the whole array make for the walls of the city. And some carried firebrands, and some scaling-ladders, and some slew the warders at the gates, and cast javelins at them who stood on the walls. And then there arose a great strife in the city, for some would have opened the gates that the men of Troy might enter, and others made haste to defend the walls. Hither and thither did they run with much tumult, even as bees in a hive in a rock which a shepherd hath filled with smoke, having first shut all the doors thereof.

Then also did other ill fortune befall the Latins, for when Queen Amata saw from the roof of the palace that the enemy were come near to the walls, and saw not anywhere the army of the Latins, she supposed Turnus to have fallen in the battle. Whereupon, crying out that she was the cause of all these woes, she made a noose of the purple garment wherewith she was clad, and hanged herself from a beam of the roof. Then did lamentation go through the city, for the women wailed and tore their hair, and King Latinus rent his clothes and threw dust upon his head.

But the cry that went up from the city came to the ears of Turnus where he fought in the furthest part of the plain. And he caught the reins and said, "What meaneth this sound of trouble and wailing that I hear?" And the false Metiscus, who was in truth his sister, made answer, "Let us fight, O Turnus, here where the Gods give us victory. There are enough to defend the city." But Turnus, spake, saying, "Nay, my sister, for who thou art I have known

even from the beginning, it must not be so.
Why camest thou down from heaven ? Was it
to see thy brother die ? And now what shall I
do ? Have I not seen Murranus die and Ufens
the Æquian ? And shall I suffer this city to
be destroyed ? Shall this land see Turnus flee
before his enemies ? Be ye kind to me, O Gods
of the dead, seeing that the Gods of heaven hate
me. I come down to you a righteous spirit, and
not unworthy of my fathers."

And even as he spake came Saces, riding on
a horse that was covered with foam, and on his
face was the wound of an arrow. And he
cried, " O Turnus, our last hopes are in thee.
For Æneas is about to destroy the city, and
the firebrands are cast upon the roofs. And
King Latinus is sore tried with doubt, and the
Queen hath laid hands upon herself and is dead.
And now only Messapus and Atinas maintain
the battle, and the fight grows fierce around
them, while thou drivest thy chariot about these
empty fields."

Then for a while Turnus stood speechless,
and shame and grief and madness were in his
soul ; and he looked to the city, and lo ! the

fire went up even to the top of the tower which he himself had builded upon the walls to be a defence against the enemy. And when he saw it, he cried, "It is enough, my sister; I go whither the Gods call me. I will meet with Æneas face to face, and endure my doom."

And as he spake he leapt down from his chariot, and ran across the plain till he came near to the city, even where the blood was deepest upon the earth and the arrows were thickest in the air. And he beckoned with the hand and called to the Italians, saying, "Stay now your arrows. I am come to fight this battle for you all." And when they heard it they left a space in the midst. Æneas also, when he heard the name of Turnus, left attacking the city, and came to meet him, mighty as Athos, or Eryx, or Father Apenninus, that raiseth his snowy head to the heavens. And the men of Troy and the Latins and King Latinus marvelled to see them meet, so mighty they were.

First they cast their spears at each other, and then ran together, and their shields struck one against the other with a crash that went up to the sky. And Jupiter held the balance in

heaven, weighing their doom. Then Turnus,
rising to the stroke, smote fiercely with his
sword. And the men of Troy and the Latins
cried out when they saw him strike. But the
treacherous sword brake in the blow. And
when he saw the empty hilt in his hand he
turned to flee. They say that when he mounted
his chariot that day to enter the battle, not heed-
ing the matter in his haste, he left his father's
sword behind him, and took the sword of
Metiscus, which, indeed, served him well while
the men of Troy fled before him, but brake,
even as ice breaks, when it came to the shield
which Vulcan had made. Thereupon Turnus
fled, and Æneas, though the wound which the
arrow had made hindered him, pursued. Even
as a hound follows a stag that is penned within
some narrow space, for the beast flees hither
and thither, and the staunch Umbrian hound
follows close upon him, and almost holds
him, and snaps his teeth, yet bites him not, so
did Æneas follow hard on Turnus. And still
Turnus cried out that some one should give
him his sword, and Æneas threatened that he
would destroy the city if any should help him.

Five times about the space they ran; not for some prize they strove, but for the life of Turnus. Now there stood in the plain the stump of a wild olive - tree. The tree was sacred to Faunus, but the men of Troy had cut it, and the stump only was left. Herein the spear of Æneas was fixed, and now he would have drawn it forth that he might slay Turnus therewith, seeing that he could not overtake him by running. Which when Turnus perceived, he cried to Faunus, saying, " O Faunus, if I have kept holy for thee that which the men of Troy have profaned, hold fast this spear." And the god heard him ; nor could Æneas draw it forth. But while he strove, Juturna, taking again the form of Metiscus, ran and gave to Turnus his sword. And Venus, perceiving it, wrenched forth the spear from the stump. So the two stood again face to face.

Then spake Jupiter to Juno, where she sat in a cloud watching the battle, " How long wilt thou fight against fate ? What purpose hast thou now in thy heart ? Was it well that Juturna—for what could she avail without thy help ?—should give back to Turnus his sword ?

Thou hast driven the men of Troy over land and sea, and kindled a dreadful war, and mingled the song of marriage with mourning. Further thou mayest not go."

And Juno humbly made answer, "This is thy will, great Father; else had I not sat here, but stood in the battle smiting the men of Troy. And indeed I spake to Juturna that she should help her brother; but aught else I know not. And now I yield. Yet grant me this. Suffer not that the Latins should be called after the name of Troy, nor change their speech nor their garb. Let Rome rule the world, but let Troy perish for ever."

Then spake with a smile the Maker of all things, "Truly thou art a daughter of Saturn, so fierce is the wrath of thy soul! And now what thou prayest I give. The Italians shall not change name, nor speech, nor garb. The men of Troy shall mingle with them, and I will give them a new worship, and call them all Latins. Nor shall any race pay thee more honour than they."

Then Jupiter sent a Fury from the pit. And she took the form of a bird, even of an owl that sitteth by night on the roof of a desolate house, and flew before the face of Turnus and flapped her wings against his shield. Then was Turnus stricken with great fear, so that his hair stood up and his tongue clave to the roof of his mouth. And when Juturna knew the sound of the false bird what it was, she cried aloud for fear, and left her brother and fled, hiding herself in the river of Tiber.

But Æneas came on, shaking his spear that was like unto a tree, and said, " Why delayest thou, O Turnus ? Why drawest thou back ? Fly now if thou canst through the air, or hide thyself in the earth." And Turnus made answer, " I fear not thy threats, but the Gods and Jupiter, that are against me this day." And as he spake he saw a great stone which lay hard by, the landmark of a field. Scarce could twelve chosen men, such as men are now, lift it on their shoulders. This he caught from the earth and cast it at his enemy, running forward as he cast. But he knew not, so troubled was he in his soul, that he ran or that he cast, for his knees tottered beneath him and his blood grew cold with fear. And the stone fell short, nor reached the mark.

Even as in a dream, when dull sleep is on the eyes of a man, he would fain run but cannot, for his strength faileth him, neither cometh there any voice when he would speak ; so it fared with Turnus. For he looked to the Latins and to the city, and saw the dreadful spear approach, nor knew how he might fly, neither how he might fight, and could not spy anywhere his chariot or his sister. And all the while Æneas shook his spear and waited that his aim should be sure. And at the last he threw it with all his might. Even as a whirlwind it flew, and brake through the seven folds of the shield and pierced the thigh. And Turnus dropped with his knee bent to the ground. And all the Latins groaned aloud to see him fall. Then he entreated Æneas, saying, " I have deserved my fate. Take thou that which thou hast won. Yet perchance thou mayest have pity on the old man, my father, even Daunus, for such an one was thy father Anchises, and give me back to my own people, if it be but my body that thou givest. Yet hast thou conquered, and the Latins have seen me beg my life of thee, and Lavinia is thine. Therefore, I pray thee, stay now thy wrath."

Then for awhile Æneas stood doubting; aye, and might have spared the man, when lo! he spied upon his shoulders the belt of Pallas, whom he had slain. And his wrath was greatly kindled, and he cried with a dreadful voice, "Shalt thou who art clothed with the spoils of my friends escape me? 'Tis Pallas slays thee with this wound, and takes vengeance on thy accursed blood." And as he spake he drave the steel into his breast. And with a groan the wrathful spirit passed into darkness.

THE END.

www.ingramcontent.com/pod-product-compliance
Lightning Source LLC
Chambersburg PA
CBHW060522030726

47498CB00004B/1037